P9-DFU-131

THE CHANGING WORLD

ARCTIC & ANTARCTIC

DAVE WELLER & MICK HART

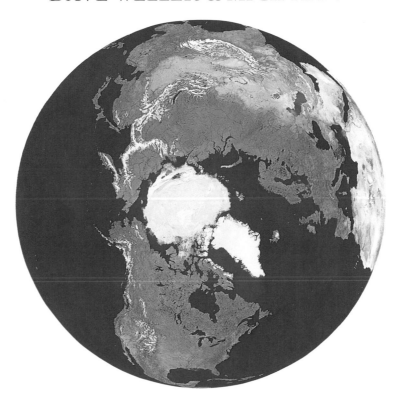

THUNDER BAY
P·R·E·S·S

ST. JOSEPH SCHOOL
275 W. North St.
Manhattan, IL 60442

Code of Safety

All activities should be conducted under adult supervision. Most of the habitats described in this series are dangerous because they are at the extremes of how our world works. They are not places you should visit without preparation or without a qualified guide. You should take suitable equipment and wear the right clothing for the environment. Take a map and a compass on all trips and learn how to use them properly. If you should find yourself in such a place through an accident, you will find some tips on how to survive there on page 60.

- **Before you go on a trip**, plan your route. **Always** tell an adult where you are going and when you expect to return.
- **Always go with a friend**, and preferably go as a party of four, which is a safe minimum number.

  If possible, go with at least one adult whom you trust—ideally someone who knows the area and the subject you are studying.
- **Ask permission** before going on to private property.
- **Leave gates closed or open** depending on how you find them. Keep off crops and avoid damaging soils, plants, animals, fences, walls, and gates.
- **Take your litter home** or dispose of it properly.
- **Remember** that many plants and animals, and their homes and habitats, are protected by law.
- **Ask your parents** not to light fires except in an emergency.
- **Beware of natural hazards** such as slippery slopes, crumbling cliffs, loose rocks, rotten tree trunks and branches, soft mud, deep water, swift currents, and tides.
- **Beware of poisonous berries**, plants, and animals: if you are not sure, don't touch them.
- Remember: **if in doubt, always play safe.**

Picture Credits

Susanna Addario: 54/55. Evi Antonio: 34; 45. Julian Baker: 6/7; 8/9; 16/17; 18; 20/21; 62/63. Bernard Thornton Artists: (Robert Morton) 52/53, 56/57; (Colin Newman) 32/33, 38/39, 46/47, 58; (David Thelwell) 42/43. IPL Inc: 55. Jeremy Light: 28 Kevin Madison: 10/11; 12/13; 24/25; 61. Adam Marshall: 22/23. Mike Saunders: 14/15; 26/27; 30/31; 64/65. Science Photo Library: (Doug Allan) 6/7, 8/9; (David Nunuk) 18; (Claude Nuridsany & Marie Perenndu) 28; (Pekka Parviainen) 18; back cover, endpapers, 1 (© Tom Van Sant, Geosphere Project, Santa Monica). Wildlife Art Agency: (Wendy Bramwell) 48/49; (Steve Roberts) 40/41; (Chris Turnbull) 36/37. Activity pictures by Mr Gay Galsworthy.

Thunder Bay Press
5880 Oberlin Drive, Suite 400
San Diego, CA 92121

First published in the United States and Canada by Thunder Bay Press, 1996

© Dragon's World Ltd, 1996
© Text Dave Weller & Mick Hart, 1996
© Illustrations by specific artists, 1996

All rights reserved

Editor	Diana Briscoe
Series Editor	Steve Parker
Designer	Martyn Foote
Art Director	John Strange
Design Assistants	Karen Ferguson
	Victoria Furbisher
DTP Manager	Michael Burgess
Editorial Director	Pippa Rubinstein

No part of this book may be reproduced or transmitted in any form or by any means, electronic or mechanical, including photocopy, recording, or any information storage and retrieval system, without permission in writing from Thunder Bay Press, except by a reviewer who may quote brief passages in a review.

Library of Congress Cataloging-in-Publication Data

Weller, Dave, 1949–
    Arctic & Antarctic : the changing world / [Dave Weller & Mick Hart].
    p. cm. — (The changing world)
    Includes index.
    Summary: Discusses such topics as the physical features, climate, plant and animal life, and environmental concerns related to the Earth's polar regions.
    ISBN 1–57145–122–6
    1. Polar regions—climate—Juvenile literature.
    2. Natural history—Polar regions—Juvenile literature.
    3. Global warming—Juvenile literature. 4. Ozone layer depletion—Polar regions—Juvenile literature.
    [1. Polar regions.   2. Natural history—Polar regions.]
I. Hart, Mick, 1949–   II. Title
III. Series: Changing world (San Diego, Calif.)
QC994.75.W47   1996
508.311—dc20

    96–5007
    CIP
    AC

Typeset by Dragon's World Ltd in Garamond, Caslon 540 and Frutiger.
Printed in Italy

Contents

The Changing World   **4**

The Ends of the World   **6**
Farthest South: Antarctica   8
Coldest Places on Earth   10
The Polar Climates   12
Seas and Currents   14
Curtains of Light   16
Sights in the Sky   18
ACTIVITY 1   19

The Poles through Time   **20**
Dinosaur Heaven   22
The Flipping Magnet   24
Ice, Ice – and More Ice   26
Snow and Ice Crystals   28
ACTIVITY 2   29

Life in the Antarctic   **30**
Teeming Southern Seas   32
Squid Galore!   34
ACTIVITY 3   35
Whales of Antarctica   36
Southern Seals   38
Plenty of Penguins   40
Sea Birds of Antarctica   42
ACTIVITY 4   44

Life in the Arctic   **45**
Arctic Whales and Seals   46
The Treeless Land   48
ACTIVITIES 5 & 6   50–51
Nesting in the North   52
Wandering the Tundra   54
Hunters of the Arctic   56
Winter Cold: Stay or Go?   58
ACTIVITIES 7 & 8   59–60

People at the Poles   **61**
Exploiting Sea and Land   62
Future Threats   64
ACTIVITIES 9 & 10   66–67

Amazing Facts   **68**

Find Out More   **70**
Glossary   **71**
Index   **72**

The Changing World of
Arctic and Antarctic

Our world, planet Earth, has never been still since it first formed—4,600 million years ago. It goes around the Sun once each year, to bring the changing seasons. It spins like a top once each day, causing the cycle of day and night. Our close companion, the Moon, circles the Earth and produces the rise and fall of the ocean tides. The weather alters endlessly, too. Winds blow, water ripples into waves, clouds drift, rain falls, and storms brew. Land and sea are heated daily by the Sun, and cool or freeze at night.

Living on the Earth, we notice these changes on different time scales. First and fastest is our own experience of passing time, as seconds merge into minutes and hours. We move about, eat and drink, learn and play, rest and sleep. Animals do many of these activities, too.

Second is the longer, slower, time scale of months and years. Many plants grow and change over these longer time periods. Return to a natural place after many years, and you see how some of the trees have grown, while others have died and disappeared.

Third is the very long, very slow time scale lasting hundreds, thousands, and millions of years. The Earth itself changes over these immense periods. New mountains thrust up as others wear down. Rivers alter their course. One sea fills with sediments, but huge earth movements and continental drift create another sea elsewhere.

The *CHANGING WORLD* series describes and explains these events—from the immense time span of lands and oceans, to the shorter changes among trees and flowers, to the daily lives of ourselves and other animals. Each book selects one feature or habitat of nature, to reveal in detail. Here you can read how cold the *ARCTIC AND ANTARCTIC* really are, and why they stay so frozen. You can find out that, despite the ice and snow, many fascinating plants and animals live there, from slow-growing mosses and lichens, to snowy owls and polar bears.

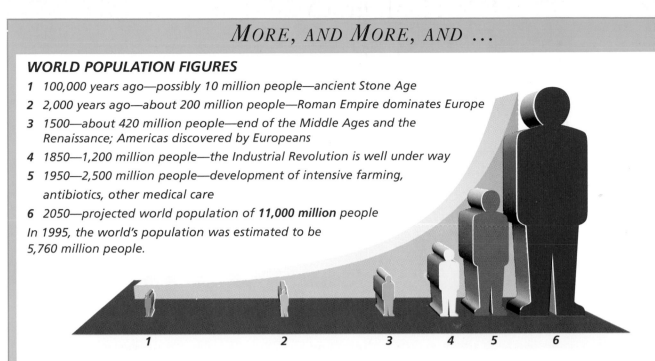

WORLD POPULATION FIGURES

1   *100,000 years ago—possibly 10 million people—ancient Stone Age*

2   *2,000 years ago—about 200 million people—Roman Empire dominates Europe*

3   *1500—about 420 million people—end of the Middle Ages and the Renaissance; Americas discovered by Europeans*

4   *1850—1,200 million people—the Industrial Revolution is well under way*

5   *1950—2,500 million people—development of intensive farming, antibiotics, other medical care*

6   *2050—projected world population of **11,000 million** people*

In 1995, the world's population was estimated to be 5,760 million people.

The most numerous large animal on Earth, by many millions, is the human. Our numbers have increased steadily from the start of civilization about 10,000 years ago speeded by advances in public health and hygiene, the Industrial Revolution, gas and diesel engines, better farming, and better medical care.

However, this massive growth in humanity means that almost half the world's people suffer from hunger, poverty and disease. The animals and plants who share our planet also suffer. As we expand our territory, their natural areas shrink ever faster. We probably destroy one species of plant or animal every week.

However, there is another type of change affecting our world. It is the huge and ever-increasing number of humans on the planet. The CHANGING WORLD series shows how we have completely altered vast areas—to grow foods, put up homes and other buildings, mine metals and minerals, manufacture goods and gadgets from pencils to washing machines, travel in cars, trains and planes, and generally live in our modern world.

This type of change is causing immense damage. We take over natural lands and wild places, forcing plants and animals into ever smaller areas. Some of them disappear for ever. We produce all kinds of garbage, waste, poisons, water and air pollution.

However, there is hope. More people are becoming aware of the problems. They want to stop the damage, to save our planet, and to plan for a brighter future. The CHANGING WORLD series shows how we can all help. We owe it to our Earth, and to its millions of plants, animals, and other living things, to make a change for the better.

An atlas shows that the polar regions extend from the Poles themselves for 1,342 miles in every direction—from the North Pole to the Arctic Circle, and from the South Pole to the Antarctic Circle. Biologists might say that the polar regions go farther. Typical Arctic weather and wildlife extend south to the line where trees grow to their full size—the "tree line" across the tundra of North America and northern Asia.

As the Earth spins through space, the Sun's rays are never strong in polar regions. This means they are the coldest places in the world. But they have not always been so cold. Ice has built up at the Poles only during the last 30 million years. It works like a global air-conditioning system to make the world's climate cooler and the Poles even colder.

The Arctic ice
The Arctic region is not land, but a relatively shallow sea. In the middle —at and near the North Pole—the surface is frozen all year round as a vast, permanent sheet of ice. It gets smaller as its edges melt back in summer, then enlarges as winter cold makes the ice sheet grow.

Smashing a path
Ice-breaking ships with strengthened hulls force a path through the edge of the Arctic ice sheet.

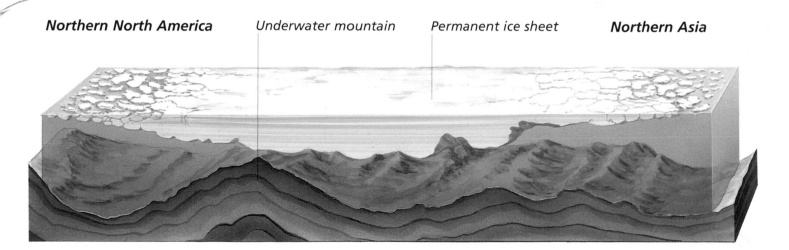

Northern North America   Underwater mountain   Permanent ice sheet   **Northern Asia**

Under the Arctic ice
The water under the ice sheet is the coldest and calmest in the world. Even though the ice is less than 33 feet thick in the middle, hardly any light passes through, so the normal plant life of the oceans, tiny algae, cannot grow. That means there is very little animal life.

The Arctic sea bed
The Arctic Ocean covers 5.5 million square miles and has an average depth of 4,365 feet, compared to the Atlantic Ocean, which measures 32 million square miles and is about 12,150 feet deep. The Arctic seabed has tall underwater mountains, ranges of hills and immense flat plains, all in pitch blackness.

Arctic to Pacific

Only two openings link the Arctic Ocean to the other oceans of the world. The Bering Sea is a shallow and very narrow passage between the Chukchi Peninsula of north-east Asia and the Seward Peninsula of Alaska. Little water flows through it, in or out of the Arctic Ocean.

Currents of ice

The pattern of water circulation in the Arctic makes the ice drift slowly, as shown by Norwegian explorer and scientist Fridtjof Nansen. For two years, 1893–95, his strengthened ship Fram drifted from eastern Siberia to Svalbard, stuck in the ice. It passed within 235 miles of the North Pole.

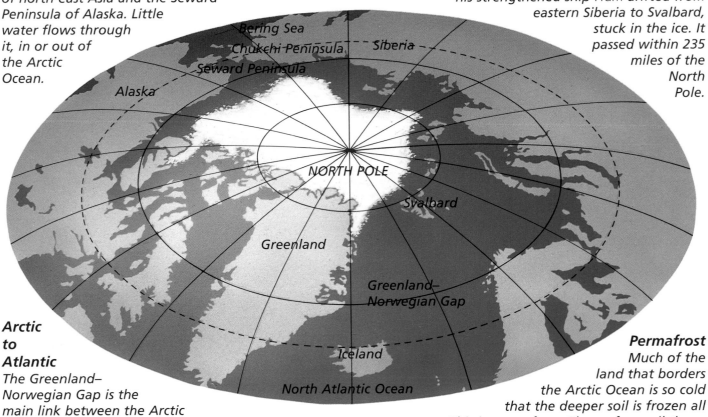

Arctic to Atlantic

The Greenland–Norwegian Gap is the main link between the Arctic Ocean and other oceans. This deep-sea passage lets warm waters of the Atlantic Gulf Stream flow north into the Norwegian Basin, to keep it virtually ice-free all year and warm the local climate.

Permafrost

Much of the land that borders the Arctic Ocean is so cold that the deeper soil is frozen all year. This is permafrost. The surface soil thaws in summer to form bogs and marshes, home to small insects such as gnats and midges, and larger animal visitors like caribou.

The Arctic is a shallow ocean rimmed by lowlands. Covered by a skin of ice, the Arctic Ocean is the coldest and calmest ocean in the world. Beneath the ice there is little life. But at the ocean's edges, where the shallow waters meet the land, and the ice melts in summer, there is a mass of sea life. Around this ocean are northern Europe, Asia and North America. Snow-bound in winter, in summer they also sustain a wealth of wildlife. The Arctic is named after the stars of Arktos, the Great Bear, which dominates the northern night sky.

ARCTIC DUCKS

In 1994 a freight container of yellow plastic bathtub ducks fell off a cargo ship near the Aleutian Islands, off Alaska, while it was sailing across the Pacific Ocean. The container broke open, and many ducks drifted north into the Bering Strait and on into the Arctic Ocean. They may get stuck in the ice and drift with its currents, or some may emerge in the Norwegian Sea in about 1998.

Farthest South: Antarctica

Antarctic means "opposite Arctic." Apart from the fact that both regions are cold, they are truly opposites. Antarctica is not an ice-covered sea, as is the Arctic—it is a mountainous continent covered by a gigantic ice sheet, with ice shelves and glaciers spilling into the surrounding ocean. Some mountain peaks break through the ice as rocky outcrops. However, most of the land is permanently covered by ice up to 14,000 feet thick.

Surrounding Antarctica, like a giant moat, is the Southern Ocean. In winter it is a frozen waste, as the ice of Antarctica spreads north across its waters. Icebergs drift relentlessly, and the surface becomes a jumbled field of broken, jagged, creaking whiteness.

However, in summer, where the ice breaks up, the Southern Ocean has the richest life of any ocean in the world. Sea birds and sea mammals, such as seals and whales, feed on millions of tons of tiny sea creatures. The influence of Antarctica on its wildlife extends north to the warmer water in the Southern Ocean, at the Antarctic Convergence.

Grow, then shrink
In winter, Antarctic sea ice extends hundreds of miles out into the Southern Ocean. The size of the ice sheet almost doubles in late winter. In photos taken from space, Antarctica appears to grow in winter, then shrink in summer.

The Southern Ocean
This is formed from the southern parts of the Atlantic Ocean, the Indian Ocean, and the Pacific Ocean. During frozen midwinter, the ice shelves spread into it from Antarctica.

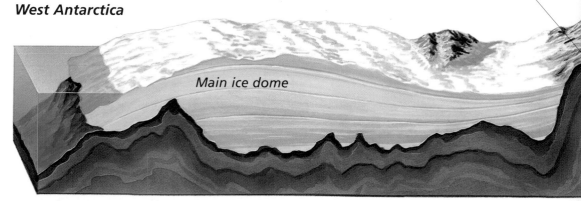

Vincennes Bay

Mackenzie Bay

Southern Indian Ocean

Rocky outcrop above ice

West Antarctica

Main ice dome

Land of Antarctica
The land mass of Antarctica is the world's fifth-largest continent, with an area of over 5 million square miles— nearly twice the area of Australia, and one-and-a-half times the size of the United States. The eastern part of Antarctica is higher. The bedrock of the western part is between 3,280 and 8,327 feet below sea level, pressed down by the weight of the ice.

Ice of Antarctica
The main ice dome is on the west side of Antarctica, where the ice is up to 14,000 feet thick. The ice in the eastern part is thinner and more irregular. Fed by snows falling on it and becoming squashed, the ice flows like a massive glacier, spilling off the land and into the surrounding seas as ice shelves.

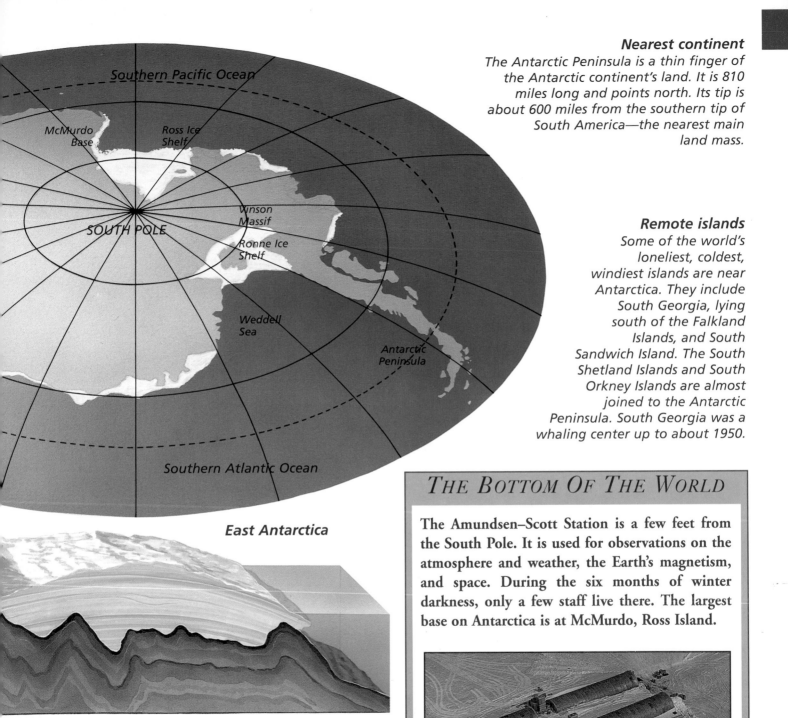

Southern Pacific Ocean

McMurdo Base

Ross Ice Shelf

SOUTH POLE

Vinson Massif

Ronne Ice Shelf

Weddell Sea

Antarctic Peninsula

Southern Atlantic Ocean

East Antarctica

Nearest continent

The Antarctic Peninsula is a thin finger of the Antarctic continent's land. It is 810 miles long and points north. Its tip is about 600 miles from the southern tip of South America—the nearest main land mass.

Remote islands

Some of the world's loneliest, coldest, windiest islands are near Antarctica. They include South Georgia, lying south of the Falkland Islands, and South Sandwich Island. The South Shetland Islands and South Orkney Islands are almost joined to the Antarctic Peninsula. South Georgia was a whaling center up to about 1950.

THE BOTTOM OF THE WORLD

The Amundsen–Scott Station is a few feet from the South Pole. It is used for observations on the atmosphere and weather, the Earth's magnetism, and space. During the six months of winter darkness, only a few staff live there. The largest base on Antarctica is at McMurdo, Ross Island.

Island mountains

A few mountains poke above the ice and form areas of exposed land. The highest is Vinson Massif at 16,066 feet, which compares with the Rockies at 14,432 feet and the European Alps at 15,770 feet. Take all the ice off Antarctica, and the loss of weight would let its land rise about 1,800 feet.

Coldest Places on Earth

The polar regions have the coldest climates on Earth. Why? As the Earth orbits, or circles, the Sun, it is tilted on its axis. The Poles are not at the top and bottom, but are slightly to the sides. For six months of the year, from September to March (the northern winter), the North Pole faces away from the Sun and is plunged in continuous darkness. At the same time, the South Pole receives continuous daylight.

From March to September (the northern summer), the situation is reversed. The South Pole is continually dark, and the Sun never sets at the North Pole. During each Pole's winter months, the Sun cannot provide any direct warmth. Yet even in the endless summer daylight, first at one Pole, then at the other, temperatures hardly rise.

There is little warmth for two reasons. First, summer weather is often cloudy, so that little direct sunlight ever reaches the surface. Second, the Sun's light and heat are reflected off bright surfaces, such as white ice. The small amount that is absorbed has

Earth and Sun
The Earth takes one year to orbit the Sun. The orbit is not an exact circle, but an ellipse, so the Earth is farther from the Sun at certain times. Coupled with the tilt of the Earth, this gives the seasons of the year.

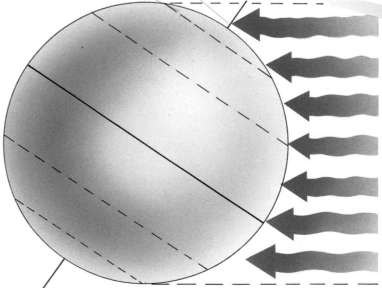

June
Midsummer in north, midwinter in south

Axis of spin

North Pole

Arctic Circle

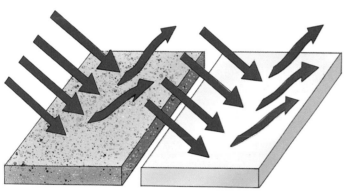

Dull rocks = low albedo   White ice = high albedo

An ice mirror
A smooth, shiny, bright surface like a mirror reflects light—and heat. This reflecting power is called the albedo. The Earth's average albedo for reflecting the Sun's light and heat is 35 per cent.

However, the white polar icecaps of Antarctica, and to a lesser extent the ice sheet of the Arctic, reflect between 50 and 90 per cent of the Sun's light and heat. This warmth goes straight back up. Some is absorbed by the atmosphere and spreads around the world. The rest goes into space. The albedo effect is one reason why the polar regions are so cold.

no great effect, especially on the high icecap of Antarctica. The ice surface averages over 6,560 feet above sea level, making Antarctica the world's highest continent. This adds to the cold, making it 22°F colder on average than the Arctic.

Only the sea ice around Antarctica, and in the Arctic along the northern coasts of Eurasia and North America, melts in summer. This is partly because of the darker background color of the ocean water beneath, which means it absorbs more warmth.

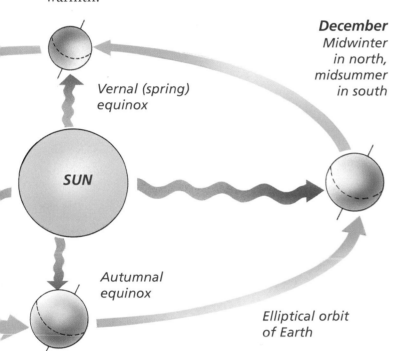

Vernal (spring) equinox

SUN

Autumnal equinox

December
Midwinter in north, midsummer in south

Elliptical orbit of Earth

Winter in the South
The lower or Southern Hemisphere is tilted away from the Sun. The South Pole gets no sunlight at all, even though the Earth spins on its axis, but the North Pole has continuous sunlight. The farthest point south that receives 24-hour sunlight at midwinter marks the Arctic Circle.

Winter in the North
As the Earth continues its orbit, the North Pole begins to turn away from the Sun. It then gets no sunlight, while it is light even at midnight below the Antarctic Circle.

HOW COLD IS COLD?

- **Near the center of Antarctica, away from the ocean's warming influence, is Russia's Vostok station, nearly 620 miles from the coast. It has the coldest average temperature in the world. In midwinter the lowest recorded temperature is –128.6°F. The highest in summer is –6°F.**

- **It is a little warmer near the coast. At Mawson Base on Greater Antarctica, the midwinter temperature is more than –4°F. It climbs just above freezing, 32°F, in midsummer.**

- **The temperature at the North Pole is around 54°F warmer than at the South Pole. The underlying ocean water, with currents from the Atlantic, has a moderating effect.**

- **In the Arctic, the only large area of ice-covered land is Greenland. Winter temperatures here fall to –40°F.**

- **London's average midwinter temperature is 39°F, while New York's is 30°F.**

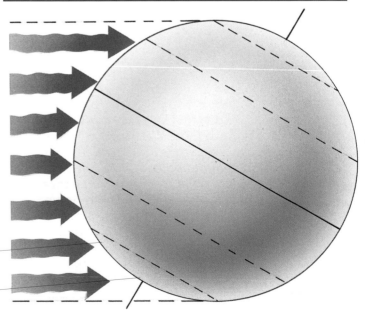

Antarctic Circle

South Pole

The Polar Climates

The polar regions are cold and remote, and they may seem to matter little to the rest of the world. But the atmosphere is like a highway for climate, linking all parts of the planet. The air of the atmosphere is always in motion. It carries weather systems around the globe, influences the temperatures and movements of ocean water, and creates the many and varied environments that support life on Earth.

Movement is a major feature of the atmosphere, and there are many forces involved. The Earth spins on its axis every 24 hours. The atmosphere is heated by day and cooled at night, causing the warmed air to rise and the cold air to fall. As the Earth spins, it drags its "floppy friend"—the atmosphere—with it, creating the Coriolis effect (see opposite). Seasons change as the Earth orbits the Sun each year. This causes different areas of air temperature and pressure in the atmosphere to move north and south.

There is an overall movement of air from warm tropical regions to cold polar zones. The Sun's warmth is greatest around its middle, near the Equator. Large quantities of surplus heat spread into the lower atmosphere and move north and south, to balance the massive loss of heat from polar regions. It is like pouring heat "straight down the sink!" This movement of heat around the world has the effect of evening out temperatures. The warm tropics prevent global freezing; the cold poles prevent global frying.

Both the Arctic and Antarctic are very dry. In fact, they are officially deserts. Nearly all their surface areas receive less than 10 inches of precipitation (snow, rain, and other forms of water) each year. In the Arctic only Iceland, Svalbard,

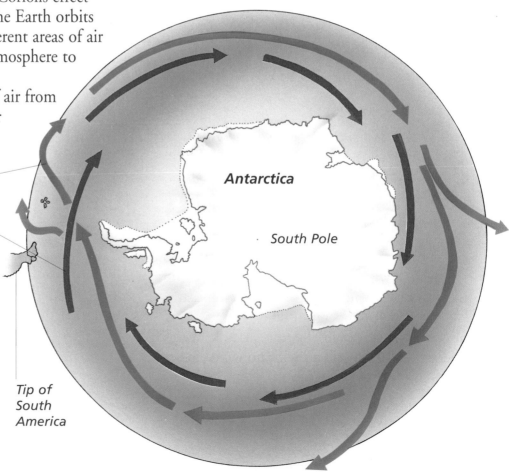

Main winter winds

Main summer winds

Southern wind patterns
The circulation of air in the Southern Ocean is dominated by westerly winds as far south as the Antarctic Circle. It is a colossal wind system that flows uninterrupted around the world. Around the coasts of Antarctica itself, the smaller local winds are mainly easterly. Local winds also form as cold, dense air rolls down the continental slope from the high Antarctic plateau.

Tip of South America

Antarctica

South Pole

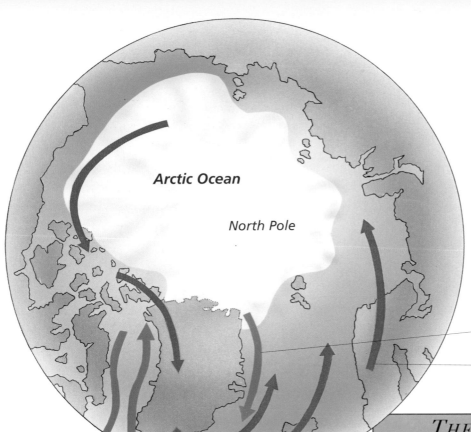

Arctic Ocean

North Pole

Northern wind patterns
Around the temperate latitudes of the Northern Hemisphere, including much of North America and Europe, the winds are generally from the west. On the northern, polar side of these westerlies, there is a marked drop in temperature, and the prevailing winds are sometimes easterly. The weather is usually cloudy, and most water falls in the form of snow. A type of fog called Arctic sea smoke is common in summer.

Main winter winds

Main summer winds

Lapland, and the southern coasts of Greenland receive more. The Antarctic Peninsula is the only part of the Antarctic continent that avoids being an official desert. Yet, more than nine-tenths of all the world's fresh water is "tied up" in the ice sheets on Antarctica and Greenland.

A local effect of weather is windchill. This is caused by high winds and low temperatures. The stronger the wind and the lower the temperature, the greater the windchill. It makes you much colder than the temperature shown by the thermometer. For example, human flesh freezes solid at −130°F, in still air with no wind. In a gale, it freezes at only 19°F. On a calm summer's day near the pole, the Sun may seem warm. But if the wind increases, it draws heat from the body, and this can kill the polar traveller.

THE CORIOLIS EFFECT

As the Earth spins, it drags the lower layers of atmosphere with it more than the upper layers. Also the speed of movement of the Earth's surface is faster towards the Equator, where the Earth is wider, than towards the Poles. These effects combine to cause regular movements of wind in the atmosphere and water in the oceans. The winds swirl and spiral in corkscrews—the Coriolis effect. The same effect makes water swirl around in a whirlpool as it goes down the plug hole.

Swirling winds
The Coriolis effect of the spinning Earth makes winds curl towards the east in temperate zones, and back again to the west towards the Poles.

Seas and Currents

In the Southern Ocean, around the temperate latitudes north of the Antarctic continent, powerful westerly winds blow towards the east. They drive the surface water in a strong eastward current. This draws in water from either side at what is called the Antarctic Convergence. As water is drawn in, some of it is forced to sink. This is "down-welling."

The down-moving water must be offset by up-moving water. Just as waters coming together causes

At the surface
In the Southern Ocean around the Antarctic continent, the winds blow mainly from west to east (see page 12). This drags at the surface water and makes it move in the same direction. Combined with the mixing, rising, and sinking effects, some waters move in a corkscrew fashion.

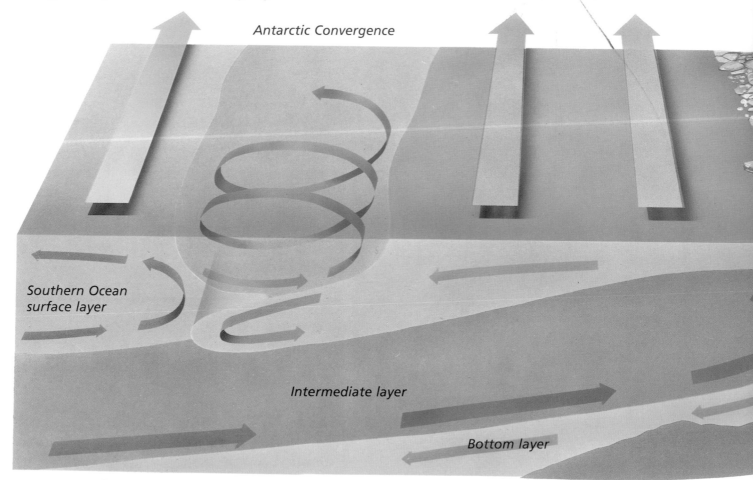

Prevailing easterly winds

Antarctic Convergence

Southern Ocean surface layer

Intermediate layer

Bottom layer

Southern Ocean surface layer
Warmer waters from the southern parts of the Atlantic, Pacific, and Indian Oceans flow near the surface.

Intermediate layer
Under the warmer waters is the cold, intermediate layer, moving steadily south to mix with the meltwater from Antarctica.

Bottom layer
This is the heaviest water in any of the world's oceans. It flows from the melted ice of Antarctica, along the seabed.

down-welling, water going in different directions causes up-welling to fill the hole that would remain.

This occurs along the Antarctic coast where prevailing offshore winds produce another region of currents, the Antarctic Divergence. The water temperature is 33°F at the surface north of the Antarctic Convergence. At the Convergence, this water merges with cold sinking water from the

continental shelf that has a temperature of −28.6°F. The merged water sinks to depths of about 13,125 feet, where it becomes Antarctic Bottom Water. This is the densest and heaviest of all ocean waters, and has a temperature of 32.7°F.

These different types and temperatures of water separate the ocean into surface, intermediate, and bottom layers. Each comes from a different source, although, over hundreds of years, the waters gradually mix together.

Meltwater
Fresh water melts from the edges of the ice shelves spilling from Antarctica, and also from the bottoms of these shelves.

Mountains of Antarctica

Rocks of Earth's crust

Antarctic Divergence
Local winds blowing offshore, from Antarctica's ice-covered land out to sea, make the surface waters move with them. This creates an up-welling, as water swirls up from below to fill the gap. Some cold meltwater from the ice shelves goes along the surface with this current, and some sinks to the sea bottom.

DOWN AND UP AGAIN

The water in the world's oceans, including the Arctic and Southern Oceans, is always on the move. Winds blow it sideways. Because of the warming effects of the Sun with the days and seasons, the water moves up and down too. These various movements recycle all the water in the world's oceans about once every 2,000 years. This means that poisons and pollutants that we dump deep in the oceans, such as radioactive wastes, may come back to the surface and cause problems hundreds of years from now.

Curtains of Light

The polar regions are famous for some of nature's most breathtaking spectacles—the auroras. They are immense, glowing curtains of light that shimmer and wave for hundreds of miles high into the atmosphere. They happen because the Sun, as well as giving out heat and light, sends out streams of rays and atomic particles, mainly electrons, known as the "solar wind."

This stream of particles is carried down through the atmosphere by the Earth's magnetic field above the magnetic poles. As the particles enter the atmosphere they begin to glow. This glow is called an aurora. It is known as the Aurora Borealis or Northern Lights in the Arctic, and the Aurora Australis or Southern Lights in the Antarctic.

The burning sky

The auroras form ghostly lights of red, violet, and green, which the Maoris of New Zealand call "the great burning of the sky." Auroras are most common and most intense near to the magnetic poles (see page 24). But they are also seen in much lower latitudes, even in Scotland, or New England.

Auroras become more intense during periods when the Sun is most active. Every eleven years, there is a "solar max," when sunspots occur more often and the solar wind is strongest. This produces the most spectacular auroras.

Old and new

For many people in the far north, life is a mixture of traditional ways—such as hunting seals through holes in the ice—and the newer Western technologies and equipment—from parkas with thermal linings to rifles and snowmobiles.

Sights in the Sky

In the skies above the polar regions, the light of the Sun or Moon produces strange and dramatic effects. The light plays on ice crystals in the lower atmosphere, and is reflected by them in many different ways. Bright edges and haloes around the Sun and Moon can appear as rings, arcs, pillars, and bright spots. Around the Sun, these are known as "sundogs," and they may be amazing colors, including all the hues of the rainbow. Around the Moon, they are usually weaker and always white.

Sunless sunrise

In winter near the pole, the Sun never rises. But it comes close to appearing above the horizon. As it does so, its rays reflect off ice crystals in the air. The glow of dawn merges with the orange of a sunset— even though the Sun is not in the sky.

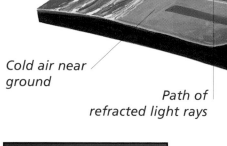

Mirage

Line of sight

Real position of horizon

Cold air near ground

Path of refracted light rays

Observer

Moon halo

The layering of air into different temperatures with different heights, and the ice crystals floating in the atmosphere, produce marvellous effects.
This Moon is surrounded by a halo formed by reflections of its own moonbeams. You may see a similar effect on a cold, clear, frosty night when the Moon is full.

Polar mirages

Mirages happen in the heat of deserts, and also near the poles. They occur close to the horizon, where the air high above the surface is slightly warmer than the freezing air just above the surface. Light rays are bent, or refracted, as they pass through the layers. Complete panoramas of coastlines, mountain ranges, icebergs, and other objects can be seen reflected as though in a mirror, suspended in the sky above the horizon. Sometimes they appear upside down.

18

Cold and Windchill

We know that polar regions are cold, but exactly how cold? Try measuring temperatures in your own area, in winter, in cold winds, and at night. Which is the lowest? How does it compare with the temperatures for polar regions on page 11? You need a maximum–minimum thermometer designed for outside use, of the type used in greenhouses, backyards, and weather stations. Find out how to set it with the small magnet, and how to take the readings. (If you can use several such thermometers, you could make all readings on the same night, which would give more accurate comparisons.)

1 Choose a week in the cold season when the forecast predicts a spell of cold weather. On the first night, leave the thermometer in an unheated room or on your porch. Note the evening temperature ten minutes after you place it there, say at 6.00 pm. When you check it next morning, say at 8.00 am, note the temperature at the time and also the minimum during the night.

2 Do the same as step 1, but put the thermometer outside. Place it in a sheltered position near a wall or in a cardboard box, out of the wind. Again, record three temperature readings.

3 Repeat the process, but place the thermometer in an exposed place outside, such as on a fence post or wall, where it will be subject to the wind and weather.

4 Take some readings after leaving the thermometer in the deep-freezer for twelve hours. Are the maximum and minimum different, indicating that the temperature inside fluctuates slightly?

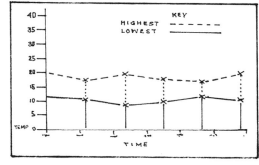

5 Draw all your results for a typical "cold night" on the chart, along with the temperature readings from page 11. Would you like to experience polar temperatures each and every night for nine months or more of the year?

The Poles through Time

The lands that lie around the Arctic and under Antarctica have been in their current positions for less than 50 million years. Many clues are evidence that the continents have wandered or drifted around the globe, over millions of years, changing the shapes of the seas between them.

The coastlines of the continents have also changed as the sea levels have gone up and down through the ages. This is due to the climate changing from wet to dry, and also water becoming locked up in ice sheets during the Ice Ages, making sea levels fall. There is evidence of ancient ice sheets and glaciers on the rocks of many lands that are now in warm zones of the Earth, including South America, Africa, Madagascar, India, and Australia.

More clues come from fossils—the preserved remains of plants and animals from

750 million years ago
The main continents were all clustered together as a supercontinent called Rodinia. Antarctica was grouped with Australia and India (all shown in green). It was only a few thousand miles from its position today—near the South Pole.

Other color codes
White – South America
Yellow – Africa and Middle East

480 million years ago
Antarctica moved north, keeping India to its south. By the Ordovician Period, it was just south of the Equator. At this time, the first fishes swam in the seas. There was no life on land.

250 million years ago
The continents continued to drift around the globe in groups. By the Permian Period, just before the Age of Dinosaurs, they had come back together to form a new supercontinent, Pangaea. Antarctica is far to the south again—joined to Africa! Northern Asia (red) and northern Europe (mauve) are at the top of the world, not far from their present positions.

For millions of years
The South Pole has been clear ocean for tens of millions of years (above), with no land and no snow. Only in the past 50 million years has the Antarctic continent arrived on the scene and become covered with ice.

prehistoric times. For instance, fossils of a small freshwater dinosaur, *Mesosaurus*, are found in western Africa and eastern South America. This led to the idea that these two continents were once joined, but then drifted apart.

Fossil-hunting on Antarctica is very difficult, because of the covering of ice. Fossils found there recently, however, show that it, too, was once a warm land with plenty of plants and animals, such as dinosaurs. Scientists believe that Antarctica, like the other continents, has been on the move for hundreds of millions of years. Once on the Equator, it has drifted south at the speed of about 1–2 inches each year, to its current position at the South Pole. The lands around the Arctic Ocean have also taken millions of years to move to their present positions.

OPPOSITE POLES

The Arctic is an ocean surrounded by continents, and the Antarctic is a continent surrounded by ocean. Yet there are similarities between the two. One is a negative or upside-down mirror-image of the other (see the maps on pages 6–9).

- Both regions have a similar surface area, about 5 million square miles.

- The Arctic Ocean's deepest point and Antarctica's highest mountain both measure about 2.5 miles from sea level.

- Antarctica's shores are steep, with few coastal flat areas, like the undersea edges of the Arctic.

- Each has a long, thin link: the Norwegian Basin connects the Arctic and Atlantic Oceans; the South Georgia Ridge links the Antarctic Peninsula to South America underwater.

Dinosaur Heaven

The land of Antarctica has a long and complicated history. Part of it is made of rocks which are among the oldest in the world, from the Precambrian Era, over 3,000 million years old. Sandstone rocks were formed on it in the Devonian Period, 400–350 million years ago, when the first tiny plants and animals were moving from the sea on to the land.

Then a major Ice Age occurred some time during the late Carboniferous and Permian Periods, 300– 250 million years ago. Following that Ice Age, a period of warm climate encouraged lots of plants to grow. These have become fossils—their remains form much of the coal that we burn today.

During the Age of Dinosaurs, especially 220–150 million years ago, Antarctica was quite different from today. It was warm, covered with green plants,

Ornithomimosaurs
These tall, slim dinosaurs ran very fast on their long back legs, very like the ostriches of today. Their beak-like mouths suggest that they probably ate a variety of foods, such as insects, leaves and shoots, and perhaps the eggs of other dinosaurs.

An Antarctic scene?
This imaginary scene from 140 million years ago is built up from evidence of fossils, especially those found in southern Australia. At the time, this region was within the Antarctic Circle. The whole world was warmer then, and especially the South Pole!

Allosaur
Fossils of this large dinosaur, which was up to 13 feet tall, show that it was a fierce hunter with many sharp teeth. It resembles Allosaurus of North America. It could probably run quite fast and slash at prey with its sharp-clawed hands.

Pterosaur
These flying creatures were not dinosaurs, but they were close relatives, members of the reptile group. They were once thought to be clumsy gliders. Many experts now believe that they were very active and skillful fliers.

and alive with animals such as dinosaurs and pterosaurs. Remains of these plants and animals have been found in South Australia, which was very near Antarctica at that time. From about 150 million years ago, there were incredible volcanic eruptions and earthquakes as the continents drifted apart once again. Over the past 100 million years, Antarctica slowly moved south once more. In the past 30 million years, it has become colder, windier, more remote, and icy—the frozen land of today.

Ankylosaur
These heavily built dinosaurs had large knobs of bones in their very thick skin for protection against meat-eaters.

Leaellynasaura
This small, slim, agile dinosaur had a very large brain for its size, and even larger eyes. Perhaps it was active at night, since the region would have had long polar nights—but without the cold.

Plants
There were few familiar blossom trees, grasses, flowers, or herbs at this time. Flowering plants had only just evolved. But there were many kinds of ferns, cycads, and conifer trees.

The Flipping Magnet

The Earth has four poles. Two are geographic—the Geographic North and Geographic South Poles. These are the usual ones we mean when we say "the Poles." They mark the line or axis around which the planet spins. The other two are the Magnetic North and Magnetic South Poles. These are formed because the Earth is like a giant magnet.

For centuries, navigators have used magnetic compasses to find the way across land and sea. The magnetic compass has an iron needle which is like a long, thin magnet. Its end marked N (North) is attracted towards the Magnetic North Pole. At the Equator, the Earth's lines of magnetic force are horizontal, and the compass works well. In the polar regions, their compasses became less reliable, as early explorers found. At the Magnetic Poles,

Earth spins around Geographic North Pole

Magnetic lines of force are vertical at the Magnetic North Pole

Crust

Mantle

Core

A giant magnet
The Earth is like a giant bar magnet with North and South Poles, surrounded by a magnetic field.
It is thought that the magnetism is generated by movements of the incredibly hot, semi-liquid rock in the mantle, deep below the surface, as the planet rotates.

North Pole

South Pole

Lines of magnetic force

Changes through time
Careful study of magnetism "frozen" into certain rocks as they form (see opposite) reveals the wanderings of the Magnetic Poles. It also shows how the magnetism has flipped or reversed over a very short time, perhaps 50–100 years. It then stayed the same for thousands or millions of years, before switching back again. This happened many times through prehistory.

the lines of force are vertical, straight down into the ground, and a compass does not work at all.

Magnetic Poles differ from the Geographic Poles in four ways. First, they are in different places—hundreds of miles away. Second, they are not exactly opposite each other, like the Geographic Poles. Third, they move very slowly over thousands of years. Fourth, they flip over occasionally so that the Magnetic North Pole becomes the Magnetic South Pole—and then they flip back again.

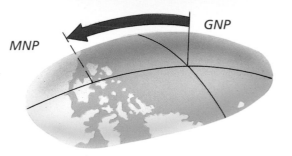

Gaps on the maps
Today, the Magnetic North Pole (MNP) lies among the Queen Elizabeth Islands in the Canadian Arctic, about 800 miles from the Geographic North Pole (GNP).

The Magnetic South Pole (MSP) lies a similar distance from the Geographic South Pole (GSP), in the Wilkes Land sector of Greater Antarctica.

Rocks move sideways

Rocks harden

North–South reversal

South–North reversal

Magnetic particles in rock

Magnetic South Pole

Magnetic rocks
Liquid or molten rock wells up from deep in the Earth through cracks, and goes solid. This happens especially at long cracks in the middle of the oceans. As certain types of rock go hard, any magnetic particles in them—which are lined up with the Earth's magnetism—become stuck or "frozen" in position. Later, the rocks twist and drift during Earth movements, and the magnetism moves with them.

Liquid rock from mantle

Magnetic Pole reversal
By studying the magnetism in rocks today, scientists can see how the layers of rocks have moved, and how the magnetic field has flipped or switched to and fro with time. This is especially clear in the rocks formed on the seabed, along cracks called mid-oceanic ridges. The magnetic particles point one way in a band of rock several hundred miles wide. Then, after a reversal, they point the other way, and so on.

25

Ice, Ice—and More Ice

Ice is not all the same. There are ice caps, ice sheets, ice shelves, ice fields, pack ice, and icebergs. How do they form? As snow falls on snow and squashes it, the light, fluffy snow on top becomes pressed into firm snow beneath. Yet more snow falls, and the firm snow below is compressed into hard ice as it gets deeper. This process has continued, uninterrupted by melting, for almost 30 million years in Antarctica. In this time, a huge amount of ice has accumulated. The Antarctic ice cap is an average of about 6,560 feet thick and in some places is more than 13,125 feet thick.

In the Arctic, the mountains of Greenland have been covered with ice for a shorter time, about

Movement of ice sheet

Flows and ridges
Sea ice calms the sea by preventing the wind from forming waves. Even so, strong winds or currents break sea ice into separate flows, with areas of open water, called leads or polynyas, between them.

Crevasses
It has been estimated that 2,000 billion tons of snow fall on Antarctica each year, adding to the total weight of the ice cap, now about 27 million billion tons. Ice slowly flows down towards the coasts. It is strained and distorted as it flows. Cracks and fissures, called "crevasses," open up.

Ice shelves
When the ice reaches the coast, it floats out onto the surface of the sea and forms an ice shelf. The biggest are in Antarctica's Ross and Weddell Seas. Each covers about 195,000 square miles and is 1,000 feet thick. Where the ice shelf faces the open sea, its cliffs are about 165 feet high. Below the surface is another 820 feet of ice.

Sea ice

As air temperatures fall from 14 to –4°F, a skin of ice crystals forms on the ocean. Any slight breeze disturbs it into "pancake" ice. Each "pancake" has raised edges as it pushes its neighbors.

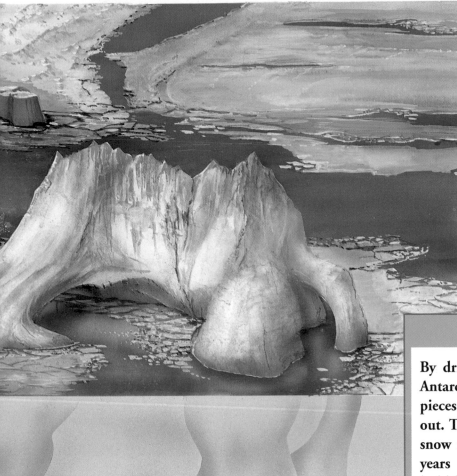

three million years. For the past 10,000 years, since the last main Ice Age, the ice has slowly retreated. The ice cap reaches 10,500 feet above sea level and covers some one million square miles.

These areas of permanent polar ice feed glaciers which flow slowly, like rivers of ice, down from the highlands towards the sea. Where ice shelves form or glaciers reach the sea, they shed huge chunks of ice—icebergs—into the water. Some Arctic icebergs are 25 miles long. Those in the Antarctic can be five times bigger. Yet along many coasts, particularly around headlands and islands, strong ocean currents help to keep the water free of ice for much of the winter.

Icebergs

The ice shelves crack and release tabular (table-like) icebergs, which drift slowly away with the ocean currents. As they move into warmer areas, they break into smaller bergs. They also get worn by the wind, waves, and currents into amazing shapes such as spires and arches.

FROZEN HISTORY

By drilling into the great ice caps of Antarctica and Greenland, long thin pieces called "ice cores" can be taken out. They are made of ice which fell as snow many hundreds or thousands of years ago. Scientists study the tiny bubbles of gas, particles of dust, pollen, fragments of insects, and other bits in the cores, to find out about changes in the world's atmosphere, climate, and wildlife.

Cores from Greenland show clear evidence of atmospheric pollution beginning in the 1700s. Those from the Antarctic are too far away to contain industrial pollution, but they hold evidence of radioactivity from the atom bomb tests in the 1950s.

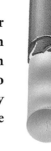

Snow and Ice Crystals

One feature is certain at both the North and South Poles—snow. It covers everything and stretches as far as you can see. The intense whiteness reflects sunlight so strongly that people wear dark glasses or goggles. Otherwise the bright whiteness hurts their eyes and they may even lose their sight for a time—a condition called "snow blindness."

Blizzards are like howling storms of snow. The snow is not usually falling snow, but loose surface snow which is then picked up, whirled around and driven by the strong winds. Polar travellers find blizzards hard to endure, calling them "whiteouts." You feel totally isolated, as in a "blackout."

Snow is made from billions of microscopic flakes, formed as water freezes high in the atmosphere. Snowflakes are always symmetrical, always beautiful, and always different. Icicles are rare, as it is hardly ever warm enough for ice to melt and drip.

There are many other types of ice crystals, too. In very calm weather, water vapor or tiny particles of ice floating in the air form sea mist. These may settle onto any slight bump on the ice floating on the water. The result is an ice flower, which looks like a fern. It can grow almost as large as your hand. In calm conditions they can grow up to 4 inches long. In the extremely still air within a crevasse, ice forms in the shape of cups or bowls (see top).

Snowflakes
Under the microscope, snowflakes always have six sides or arms. No two have ever been seen that are exactly the same.

Ice garden
The very still and ultra-cold conditions inside a crevasse allow all kinds of ice formations to form. Tiny floating crystals make a branching pattern like a fern or a tree.

The Power of Ice

As water freezes into ice, it gradually gets larger, or expands. The power of the expansion is terrific, as shown below. It can easily split stones and rocks. This is why the landscape in some polar regions, where the temperature goes above and below freezing daily, is worn away so quickly. You can also see how icebergs float mostly below the water, making them very dangerous to ships and boats. You need a large and approximately cube-shaped plastic box with a push-on lid, such as a sandwich box or ice cream carton, and also some stiff card, glue, a waterproof pen or a pencil, a large bowl of water, and the use of a deep freezer.

1 Cut out three strips of card so that they are the same length as each side of the plastic box—height, width and depth. With a pen or pencil, draw a scale with lines 1/4 inch apart on each strip. Fix them in position inside with small blobs of glue, all from the same corner of the box, and with the scales facing the plastic side, not into the box.

2 Fill the plastic box completely with water and push on the lid. Place it in the deep freezer overnight.

3 Take out the box next morning. See how the water expanded as it froze. It may have pushed the lid off the box and even cracked the plastic, too.

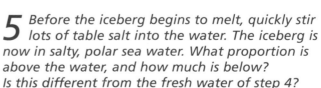

4 Remove the block of ice, which is now an iceberg in a cold northern lake. Place it in a large bowl of cold, fresh water. It may turn over, but you have scales along each edge, so this does not matter. Count how many divisions are above the surface and how many are below. How much of the iceberg floats?

5 Before the iceberg begins to melt, quickly stir lots of table salt into the water. The iceberg is now in salty, polar sea water. What proportion is above the water, and how much is below? Is this different from the fresh water of step 4?

Life in the Antarctic

In Antarctica, the only areas that are not covered by ice all the year round are the tops of the mountain peaks, a few "dry valleys" and some coastal areas of the continent and its offshore islands. The rest, more than 97 per cent, is always covered by ice. The ice-free land of the Antarctic is cold, dry and windy—a polar desert. It is very difficult for plants and animals to thrive there. Yet, despite the harsh conditions, there are some forms of life. They depend on the thin, sparse soil which has formed over the past few thousand years.

The first stages of soil formation involve the breaking of surface rocks into smaller and smaller pieces—gravel, coarse sand, then fine sand, silt, and finally, the tiniest particles of clays and muds. Wind and water act on these particles to form mineral soil which can hold small amounts of moisture. Simple plants such as algae, and microbes like bacteria, take a hold and begin to enrich the soil. Their dead

Lichens
Lichens are not true plants. They are combinations of a type of plant, algae, and fungi—the group which includes molds, mushrooms, and toadstools. Lichens have no roots. They absorb minerals and nutrients from rain. They grow very, very slowly on the rocks, in rough-looking patches of greens, yellows, and browns.

Mosses
There are thick mats of mixed mosses, algae, and lichens in the slightly warmer, damper areas on the coasts of the Antarctic Peninsula, on nearby islands, and in the glasshouse-like shelter of snow banks. Mosses are simple plants without proper leaves, roots, or flowers. They can withstand being frozen and they breed by means of spores, not seeds. They are also very small, rarely more than 2 inches tall.

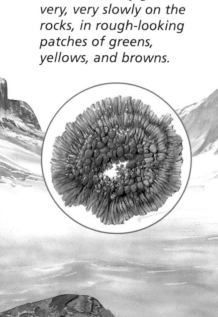

bodies rot to form a spongy, nutrient-rich substance, humus, that helps the soil to hold more moisture. In turn, this provides a base for more plants to grow.

Very few areas of Antarctica have developed beyond the mineral soil stage. The freezing and thawing, the rapid break-up of surface rocks, very low temperatures and moisture levels, and high winds carrying ice particles which blast the land, all mean that much of Antarctica's mineral soil has no life. Yet here and there in sheltered valleys, especially around the coast, some hardy life-forms survive. Antarctica has a few hundred species of algae and lichens, fewer than a hundred species of moss, and only two species of flowering plants. The animals are mainly tiny plant-eaters, such as insects, which pass most of the year as freeze-resistant eggs.

Carnivores

With so few herbivores, there is hardly any food for land-based Antarctic meat-eaters. To match the wolves and foxes of the Arctic, the Antarctic has only pinhead-sized carnivorous mites. They are the "top predators" of the whole region. They feed on other tiny mites and insects.

Herbivores

The sparse, slow-growing plants mean that there are no large Antarctic land herbivores to compare with the caribou of the Arctic. There are tiny insects, such as springtails, and the miniature relations of spiders called mites.

Flowers

In most habitats, flowering plants are the main plant life. They include most familiar grasses, trees, bushes, flowers, and herbs. But the continent of Antarctica has only two types. They are a grass, Deschampsia antarctica, *and a type of small flower called a pink,* Colobanthus quitensis.

Teeming Southern Seas

All animals depend on plants, either directly or indirectly, for food. In polar regions, the main plants growing in the water are billions of microscopic algae, especially diatoms. As with larger plants such as flowers and trees, these diatoms depend on three essentials: the gas carbon dioxide, light, and mineral nutrients.

Low temperatures allow more carbon dioxide to be dissolved in water, so polar oceans have plenty of this gas (even more than tropical seas). What about light? The Arctic and Antarctic are dark in their winters. In summer they have sunlight for up to 24 hours each day—but only if the light can reach the plants. If the sea is covered by ice, like much of the Arctic Ocean, and the southern parts of the Ross and Weddell Seas in Antarctica, little light gets through to the water beneath. So the tiny diatom plants cannot grow well.

The third essential, mineral nutrients, is very abundant, particularly in the Southern Ocean around Antarctica. The waters there are constantly fed with nutrients by a deep current which wells up from below, bringing minerals and other substances (see page 14.) So during the summer months, especially in the well-lit waters around the ice shelves and islands, the water turns green because of the vast numbers of diatoms. These microscopic plants are the basic food for tiny animals, who are in turn eaten by bigger ones, and then by the biggest of all, as shown on the following pages.

Ice fish
This hunting fish is about two feet long and feeds on other fish, shrimps, prawns, and similar animals. It has a natural, chemical "antifreeze" in its blood, which prevents its body from freezing even when the water temperature is well below freezing. It is also unusual because its blood is not red but whitish, like watery milk.

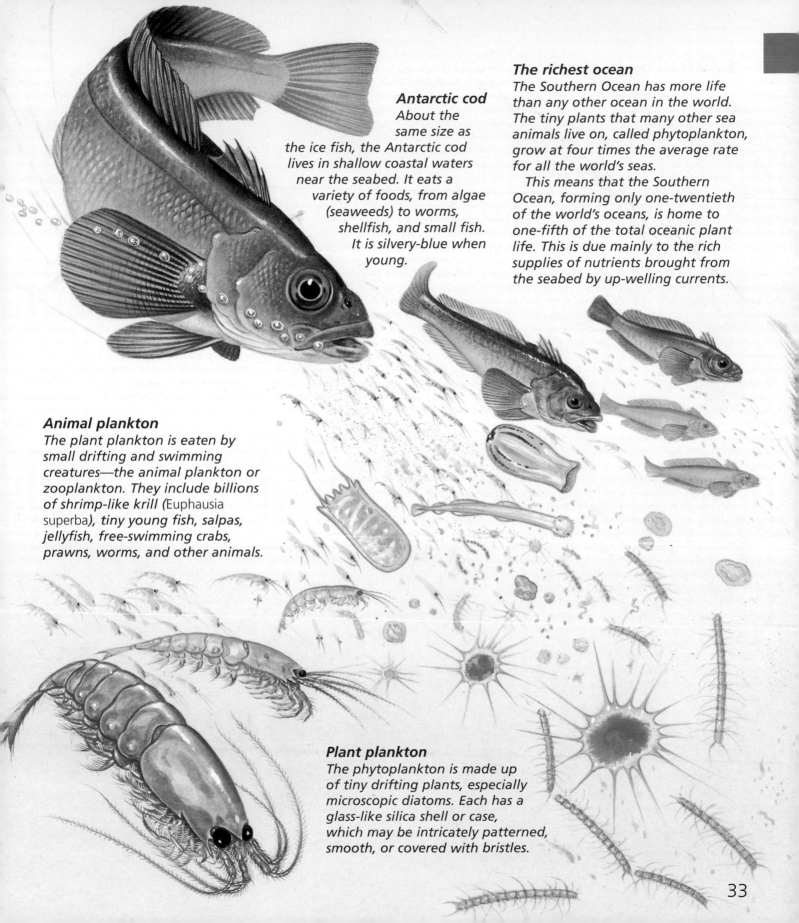

Antarctic cod
About the same size as the ice fish, the Antarctic cod lives in shallow coastal waters near the seabed. It eats a variety of foods, from algae (seaweeds) to worms, shellfish, and small fish. It is silvery-blue when young.

The richest ocean
The Southern Ocean has more life than any other ocean in the world. The tiny plants that many other sea animals live on, called phytoplankton, grow at four times the average rate for all the world's seas.

This means that the Southern Ocean, forming only one-twentieth of the world's oceans, is home to one-fifth of the total oceanic plant life. This is due mainly to the rich supplies of nutrients brought from the seabed by up-welling currents.

Animal plankton
The plant plankton is eaten by small drifting and swimming creatures—the animal plankton or zooplankton. They include billions of shrimp-like krill (Euphausia superba), tiny young fish, salpas, jellyfish, free-swimming crabs, prawns, worms, and other animals.

Plant plankton
The phytoplankton is made up of tiny drifting plants, especially microscopic diatoms. Each has a glass-like silica shell or case, which may be intricately patterned, smooth, or covered with bristles.

Squid Galore!

Sharp beak
The squid has a sharp, beak-like mouth in the middle of its ring of tentacles. It can snip through the scales of fish and the shells of shellfish.

Eyes
A squid's eyes are large and sensitive to shapes, patterns, and movements. These animals signal to each other by making their body colors change in flashes and waves of light and dark.

In the darkness of winter, the animals of the plankton sink into the warmer waters, 820 to 6,560 feet below the surface. Here they pass the winter, beyond the reach of birds, seals, and whales. As the plant plankton begin to grow again, in the warmth and light of spring, the planktonic creatures come back up to the surface to feed again. Because the plant plankton is richest in areas of up-welling nutrients, so is the animal plankton, and so are the larger animals that feed on them. One of these, both in the Antarctic and Arctic, is the squid.

This slim, fast-swimming cousin of the octopus has large eyes and sees well. It grasps food with its two longer, suckered tentacles and is a fierce hunter, eating krill and any smaller animals it can catch. It can jet along by squirting water from beneath its cloak-like outer body layer, the "mantle."

Some squid species are smaller than your little finger, others are longer than your arm. They swarm in millions, feeding, fighting, and mating in the polar seas. They provide huge amounts of food for sea birds, penguins, seals, and whales.

Feathers, Fur, and Blubber

Many warm-blooded polar creatures have an outer insulating layer that keeps the cold conditions out and body heat in, such as feathers or long, thick fur. But these do not work so well when wet. So many animals that swim, such as penguins, seals and polar bears, also have a layer of blubber, like fatty jelly, under the skin. Evolution has caused whales to lose their fur and rely solely on the blubber. For this project, you need four large ice cubes and three outer layers of insulation, as follows.

1 Make a bird's outer covering by cutting feather shapes from soft tissue paper, and gluing their shafts to a piece of flat paper. The feathers should overlap each other so that any part of the feathery coat is at least five feathers thick, as in a real bird.

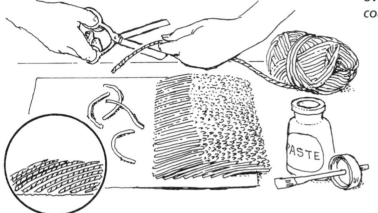

2 Make a musk ox's fur coat on a similar piece of flat paper, by gluing lengths of knitting wool to it. Again, ensure that the bases of the fur or hair are close together, so that they overlap many times to give a coat that is very thick.

3 For blubber, take a small waterproof plastic bag and part-fill it with cooking oil. When you wrap this around the ice cube, use Scotch® tape so that the oily layer is distributed in a fairly constant thickness all around the cube.

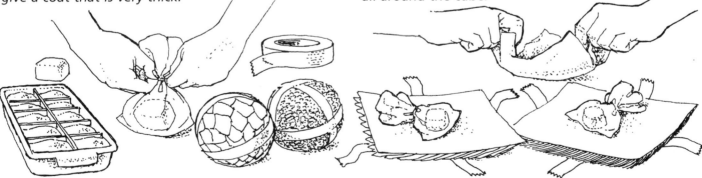

4 Take the ice cubes from the freezer and wrap each one tightly in a plastic bag, to prevent water leaking out as they melt. Quickly wrap three in the three insulating coats as detailed above. Wrap the fourth in a plain piece of flat paper.

5 The insulating coats are working in the opposite way to the real ones—they prevent cold from escaping. But the principle and the result are the same. Which ice cube melts first? Would a double thickness of blubber and fur be even more effective?

Whales of Antarctica

No ocean has as many whales, or as many different whales, as the Southern Ocean around Antarctica. There are two main whale groups. The toothed whales are hunters, mainly agile swimmers that can dive to great depths in search of prey. The baleen whales have large, flat, hairy-edged plates of whalebone (baleen) hanging from the upper jaw. They fill their mouths with sea water and plankton, and then squeeze the water out through the baleen plates and swallow the trapped plankton.

Many of the biggest whales—like the blue, humpback, and sperm whales—are found in both Antarctic and Arctic waters. However these are separate groups or populations of the same species. The general pattern is for these animals to swim away from the Pole as winter approaches, on a long-distance migration towards the warmer but food-poor waters of the tropics. They stay there and the pregnant females give birth. Then in the spring,

Pods
Killer whales live in family groups called pods. They work together to round up their prey such as fish or seals.

Killer whale (orca)
The killer whale is well named. At 20–26 feet in length, 3–6 tons in weight, and with a fearsome array of teeth, it attacks and eats fish, seals, birds, squid, and other whales. Killer whales have even been known to attack the much larger blue whales. They also ride the surf into the shore to grab unsuspecting seal pups or young sea birds, then turn and wriggle back into the water.

they head towards the Pole again, with their young, to feed on the summer abundance of food.

However, when it is summer in the north, the northern whales are feeding around the Arctic, while the southern whales are in the tropics south of the Equator. So the northern and southern groups of the same whale species probably never meet or mix.

Whale migrations

As autumn approaches, the large whales begin their long journey from polar waters to tropical seas. Humpback whales may swim more than 3,100 miles—and the same again on the return journey next spring.

Minke whale

Smallest of the baleen whales, the minke is 26 feet long and weighs up to 8 tons.
It feeds on krill and small fish. There are some 400,000 in the Southern Ocean and 125,000 in the north.

Fin whale

The fin whale is the second biggest of all animals, after the blue whale. It averages 69 feet in length and may weigh up to 75 tons. Unlike blues, fins rarely feed close to the ice edge but, like the blues, they feed on krill and any other animals in the plankton. There are now about 500,000 fin whales—only one-quarter of the number that existed before commercial whaling began.

THE DEEPEST DIVER

Only large male sperm whales venture far north and south, into the very coldest polar seas. These are the largest of the toothed whales. The males, or bulls, may reach 66 feet long and weigh 50 tons. The sperm whale feeds mainly on squid and fish. It can dive deeper than any other mammal, perhaps 10,000 feet below the surface.

Southern Seals

Seals, like whales, are mammals. They breathe air, are warm-blooded, and feed their babies on mother's milk. While they live much of their lives in the sea, eating and resting there, they have to come out of the water on to ice or land to mate, give birth and suckle their young. There are six kinds or species of seals in the waters around Antarctica. Five of these are true seals—the crabeater, Weddell, southern elephant, Ross, and leopard seals. The sixth Antarctic seal is the southern fur seal, which is related to the sea lions.

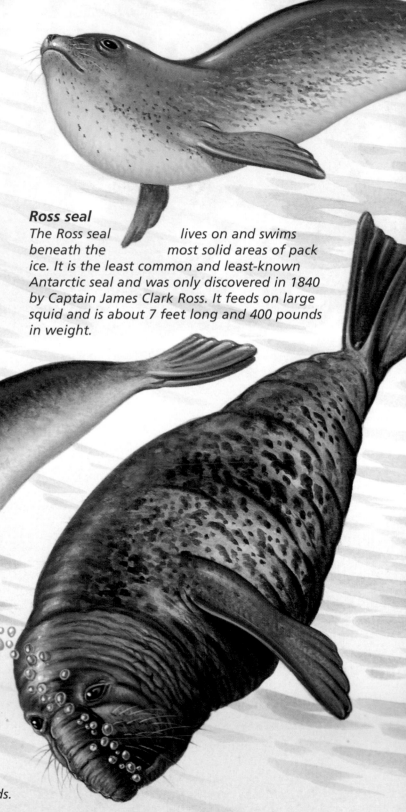

Ross seal
The Ross seal lives on and swims beneath the most solid areas of pack ice. It is the least common and least-known Antarctic seal and was only discovered in 1840 by Captain James Clark Ross. It feeds on large squid and is about 7 feet long and 400 pounds in weight.

Crabeater seal
The most abundant seals in the world, with a population of about 15 million, crabeaters live and breed on the edge of the pack ice all around Antarctica. Despite its name, the crabeater eats krill and other crustaceans using comb-like teeth. It is about 8.5 feet long and weighs about 510 pounds.

Southern elephant seal
The world's largest seal molts, mates, and breeds on the northern end of the Antarctic Peninsula, and on nearby islands and the shores of South America. This seal gets its name from its great size and the long, trunk-like nose of the adult male. He grows to about 15 feet long and 8,800 pounds in weight. Females are smaller: 10 feet, weighing 2,000 pounds.

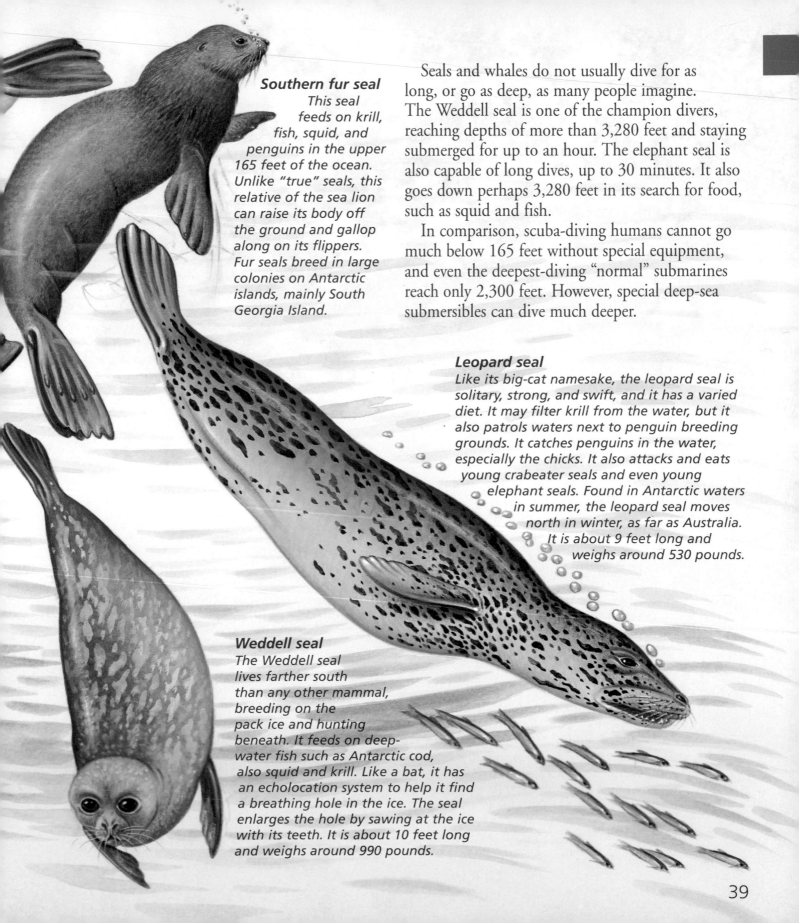

Southern fur seal
This seal feeds on krill, fish, squid, and penguins in the upper 165 feet of the ocean. Unlike "true" seals, this relative of the sea lion can raise its body off the ground and gallop along on its flippers. Fur seals breed in large colonies on Antarctic islands, mainly South Georgia Island.

Seals and whales do not usually dive for as long, or go as deep, as many people imagine. The Weddell seal is one of the champion divers, reaching depths of more than 3,280 feet and staying submerged for up to an hour. The elephant seal is also capable of long dives, up to 30 minutes. It also goes down perhaps 3,280 feet in its search for food, such as squid and fish.

In comparison, scuba-diving humans cannot go much below 165 feet without special equipment, and even the deepest-diving "normal" submarines reach only 2,300 feet. However, special deep-sea submersibles can dive much deeper.

Leopard seal
Like its big-cat namesake, the leopard seal is solitary, strong, and swift, and it has a varied diet. It may filter krill from the water, but it also patrols waters next to penguin breeding grounds. It catches penguins in the water, especially the chicks. It also attacks and eats young crabeater seals and even young elephant seals. Found in Antarctic waters in summer, the leopard seal moves north in winter, as far as Australia. It is about 9 feet long and weighs around 530 pounds.

Weddell seal
The Weddell seal lives farther south than any other mammal, breeding on the pack ice and hunting beneath. It feeds on deep-water fish such as Antarctic cod, also squid and krill. Like a bat, it has an echolocation system to help it find a breathing hole in the ice. The seal enlarges the hole by sawing at the ice with its teeth. It is about 10 feet long and weighs around 990 pounds.

Plenty of Penguins

Chinstrap penguin
The chinstrap is similar in size to the Adélie penguin, and feeds on krill. Its breeding range is more northerly, but partly overlaps with that of the Adélie penguin. On some islands off the Antarctic continent there are huge mixed colonies of the two species.

Penguins are birds—but they cannot fly. Instead, they are superb swimmers and divers, and their wings are perfectly adapted for "flying" under the water. Penguins are also adapted to the cold, and they cannot survive in the warm waters of the tropics. All of them live in the Southern Hemisphere, on and around Antarctica. There are no penguins in the Arctic and so, in nature, they never meet polar bears or walruses.

Emperor penguin
This is the largest penguin, 45 inches tall and weighing up to 88 pounds. All its breeding colonies are on the sea ice along the shores of the Antarctic continent. These birds seldom venture into sub-Antarctic waters. They feed mainly on fish, caught during dives to depths of 820 feet and lasting 15 minutes.

King penguin
With its golden breast feathers, orange head patches and orange bill, this is the second largest penguin. It is about 27 inches tall and weighs about 26 pounds. Kings are fish- and squid-feeders and may dive to depths of 650 feet. They lay their eggs in spring and the chicks hatch in summer. Unlike other penguins, the chicks take a year or more to become independent, so king penguins do not breed every year.

There was an attempt by people to introduce penguins into the Arctic. However, the experiment failed, and all the penguins died. This was perhaps fortunate for the Arctic and its natural wildlife (but unfortunate for the penguins involved.)

There are 16 species of penguins, but only two are truly Antarctic, regularly visiting and breeding on the continent itself. These are the emperor and Adélie penguins. Female emperor penguins lay a single egg, not in spring like almost every other bird, but at the beginning of the coldest part of the winter. The egg is cared for and kept warm by the male, who places it on top of his feet, covered by a fold of his body skin and feathers. The males of the colony huddle together like this through the dark, bitter cold and blizzards of the Antarctic winter, while the females feed at sea. When the egg hatches, the female returns to feed her chick and the male goes to sea. He may lose almost half his body weight while tending the egg.

Adélie penguins spend winter at sea. They return to their rocky-shore breeding colonies by travelling many miles across sea ice. They lay a pair of eggs, incubate them and rear the chicks during the short summer, between November and February.

Macaroni, rockhopper and king penguins are all birds of the sub-Antarctic. Some penguins eat krill, and when mass whaling reduced the numbers of krill-feeding whales, the krill-eating penguins increased. For example, there are probably about 10 million chinstrap penguins.

Gentoo penguin
The biggest gentoo breeding colonies are on the remote island of South Georgia, but their overall range is similar to that of the chinstrap. Gentoo penguins feed on krill and fish, and their numbers are estimated at 350,000. No penguin species are threatened with extinction in the Antarctic.

Adélie penguin
The Adélie is a penguin of the far south, with breeding colonies on the rocky shores of the Antarctic continent and its nearby islands. It stands about 20 inches high and weighs 11 pounds. Adélies feed on krill and fish which they catch in the plankton-rich surface waters.

41

Sea Birds of Antarctica

Dove prion
The dove or Antarctic prion catches plankton as it flies and dips over the water's surface. It breeds in burrows on sub-Antarctic islands and has a wingspan of around 2 ft.

Most of the middle of the Antarctic continent is covered in ice and snow, with no food or shelter. So it is little used by birds who wish to feed or breed, apart from penguins, and there is only the occasional bird visitor. But the nearby islands and the surrounding waters of the Southern Ocean are home to dozens of species of sea birds.

Petrels are truly birds of the ocean—they only come ashore to breed. They have characteristic tube-shaped structures on their beaks which help to get rid of the excess salt in sea water and in their food. Like other birds with this feature, they belong to the "tube-nose" bird group. Petrels are superb fliers, but clumsy on land. If approached by another animal or a person, many petrels "throw up" and regurgitate their food as a defence.

Wilson's storm petrel is probably the commonest sea bird in the world. Yet its breeding grounds are in the Antarctic, and it spends much of its life

Southern giant petrel
This scavenger feeds on seal and bird carcasses on land, as well as krill, fish, and squid across the Southern Ocean. Its breeding grounds on the Antarctic Peninsula and nearby islands are often close to penguin colonies. During the summer, as these huge birds feed their young, half their food may be penguin chicks.

Blue-eyed shag
Feeding close to the Antarctic Peninsula and its islands, these sea birds often fly, swim, and dive together. They eat fish, but also take squid, crabs, and other animals on the shallow seabed.

Snow petrel
This bird of the far south has pure-white plumage, black eyes and bill, and a wingspan of about 30 inches. Like the Antarctic petrel, it feeds on krill and small fish among the pack ice. It nests in rock crevices on the inland peaks and coastal cliffs of Antarctica and surrounding islands.

Brown skua
Looking like large brown gulls, brown skuas are the pirates of the sub-Antarctic region. They steal food from other birds, take their eggs and chicks, and even dig up their nest burrows to eat the young. Skuas defend their territories fiercely, attacking anything that approaches them, including people, who get pecked on the head!

Antarctic terns
These dainty birds breed on the northern Antarctic Peninsula and on sub-Antarctic islands. They feed on small fish and krill in the manner of all terns, by fluttering above the surface and dipping in their beaks.

Antarctic fulmar
The Antarctic fulmar looks like a gull and feeds on fish and squid. It is a large bird, with a wingspan of 4 feet. These fulmars nest in huge colonies on cliffs on the Antarctic Peninsula and islands of the Scotia Sea.

wandering the oceans—which means that most people will never see one. These small petrels feed on krill, and nest all around the coast of Antarctica in burrows in moss banks, in rock crevices, and out in the open.

There are also several kinds of skuas around Antarctica. McCormick's skua is the most southerly bird in the world. Much of its diet is fish and krill, caught on the surface of the sea. Like the brown skua, it takes the eggs and chicks of other bird species, and it also harasses birds to steal their food.

Signs in the Snow

Like the soft mud at the edge of a pond or river bank, or the wet sand of a seashore, the snows of polar regions make excellent records of the animals who pass over them. There are footprints, tail drags, and peck marks, urine stains, and droppings are also easier to see.

But you do not have to go to the poles to track these creatures, if you have snow in your area. After a fresh snowfall on a cold day, see how many prints you can recognize. Their sequence and the distance between them show if the animal was walking, running, or leaping.

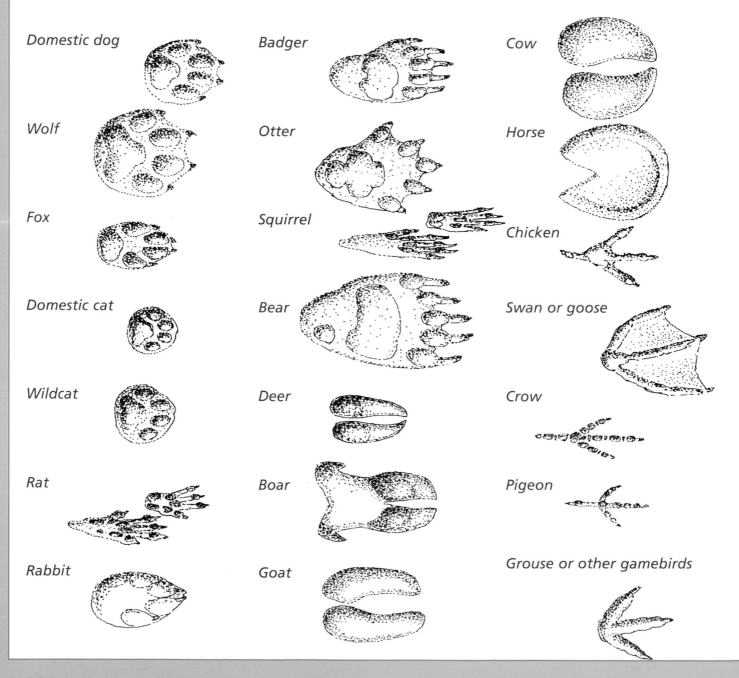

Domestic dog

Wolf

Fox

Domestic cat

Wildcat

Rat

Rabbit

Badger

Otter

Squirrel

Bear

Deer

Boar

Goat

Cow

Horse

Chicken

Swan or goose

Crow

Pigeon

Grouse or other gamebirds

As in the Antarctic, the basic food of Arctic Ocean creatures is the tiny, drifting plant plankton. This is eaten by tiny animals such as copepods and larger, finger-sized krill (euphausids). However, life in the high Arctic is sparse. Little light passes through the floating ice sheet, so there are only small quantities of plant plankton below it. Also, currents and winds cannot stir the ocean to bring nutrient-rich water up from the depths.

Only on the edges of the Arctic—especially in the Barents Sea north of Russia, around the Canadian islands, and off Greenland—does the ice break up in spring, and ocean currents bring deep, mineral-rich water to the surface. This allows plant plankton to thrive. It is eaten by animal plankton, then by larger fish including Arctic cod, Arctic char, and capelin. The plankton and fish feed sea birds, seals, and many kinds of whales. Bearded seals and walruses search in the mud of the shallow waters around the edges of the Arctic Ocean for shellfish and similar food.

Walrus

The walrus is found in shallow waters, or hauled out on ice floes or the shore, along the coasts of northern Canada, Greenland, Iceland, and the Kara and Barents Seas. Males weigh about 1.5 tons and grow to 11.5 feet in length. The male's tusks may grow to 3 feet, those of the female to 2 feet. The walrus grubs in the mud for clams and other shellfish, crabs, worms, and other sea life.

Arctic Whales and Seals

Like the Antarctic, the Arctic has many species of seals and whales. There are seven Arctic seals. Six, including the walrus, are true seals, while the northern fur seal, like its southern cousin, is related to the sea lions. There are also northern populations of baleen (whalebone) whales such as the blue, fin, and humpback. They migrate from the polar waters to the tropics as winter approaches, like their counterparts in the Antarctic. A type of baleen whale found only in the Arctic is the bowhead.

Among the toothed whales, older male sperm whales venture right to the edge of the floating Arctic ice raft and even beneath it, but the females and young stay in the slightly less cold, sub-Arctic waters. Like the sperm whale, the northern bottlenose whale has sharp teeth and is a swift hunter. It is found in the North Atlantic and in Arctic waters around Greenland and Svalbard, hunting for squid in deep water. It can dive to 3,000 feet and remain submerged for an hour. Males grow to 33 feet, females about 3 feet less.

Narwhal
This strange tusked animal may have produced the myth of the unicorn. One of its upper teeth grows into a spiral tusk up to 10 feet long. The whale itself is about 15 feet long and weighs 2,000 pounds.

Ringed seal
This seal lives all year among the Arctic pack ice and in the Bering Sea, North Pacific, and North Atlantic. It is also found in freshwater lakes in north-western Europe. It feeds on fish and crustaceans. This species has always been hunted by the native peoples of the Arctic. It is thriving, with a total population of up to 6 million.

Beluga
The beluga or white whale also lives only in the Arctic (although there is also a small group in the Gulf of St. Lawrence). Males grow to about 15 feet long and weigh 1.5 tons, females are slightly smaller. They feed mainly on fish.

Harp seal
These seals live on Arctic offshore ice, in the Greenland and Barents Seas, and off the Labrador coast. Adults grow to about 400 pounds and 6 feet in length. They eat fish and crustaceans. Like ringed seals, harp seals have been hunted by Arctic peoples for thousands of years. Mass hunting began in the 18th century and stopped in 1987.

Bowhead whale
This huge and bulky whale, 50 feet long, is restricted to Arctic waters. Bowheads have very fine baleen (whalebone) and can filter very small items from the plankton. They swim slowly, straining water through their baleen plates, swallow, and repeat the process.

Northern fur seal
These eared seals breed on tiny islands between Alaska and the Kamchatka Peninsula in the summer. They rest on land by day, and hunt fish and squid at night. In autumn they migrate south, as far as San Diego or Tokyo. They grow to about 7 feet in length and are a favorite food of killer whales.

47

The Treeless Land

Unlike the Antarctic, the Arctic has vast areas of surrounding land where life can thrive—at least during the short summer. The more southerly lands of the Arctic have been largely free of permanent ice for 10,000 years, since the last Ice Age. This has allowed soils to develop, and many thousands of plant species make their home in the region. New, young plants grow well in the shelter provided by existing plants, and so more species are constantly arriving from the temperate lands to the south and becoming suited to the local conditions. This is why many Arctic plants are closely related to species which grow in the temperate zones to the south.

On the Arctic land, between the conifer trees of the northern forests and the shores of the Arctic Ocean, there are two main kinds of environments, each with its own wildlife. These are the tundra (meaning "treeless land") and the polar desert. The tundra merges into the polar desert, where the average summer temperature falls to about 43°F.

The tundra begins
Forest ends and tundra begins at the tree line, where the average summer temperature is 50°F. The tundra is frozen solid for eight months each year, but it rapidly becomes waterlogged in spring as the temperature rises and the snows melt. There are many patches of reindeer moss, which is really algal plants and fungi growing together.

Arctic poppy and Arctic fritillary
The Arctic fritillary has similar beautiful, intricate wing patterns to its fritillary cousins farther south, and it searches for nectar. The Arctic poppy grows in the more stony, better drained areas.

Water beetle
As the meltwater forms pools and streams, these come alive with small creatures. The larvae of mosquitoes and other insects hatch out, and are eaten by hunters such as diving beetles.

In the polar desert of the Arctic Ocean's coast and nearby islands, soils are thin and sparse. Half the land has no plant life. The plants that survive in the other half are small, stunted by the short summer growing season, bitter winters, and lack of moisture—most water is frozen into ice. Where the temperature averages 36°F or below, only the hardiest plants can survive, such as mosses and the plant-fungus partnerships known as lichens.

Yet this Arctic polar desert has far more wildlife than the entire mainland of Antarctica.

On the tundra in spring, the water melts to form huge marshes. The air is soon full of insects, as clouds of midges, gnats, and mosquitoes plague the larger animals such as caribou or reindeer that visit the region for summer. These tiny creatures also represent a great food source, particularly to the birds that migrate north for the summer.

Mosquitoes, gnats and midges

Vast swarms of these tiny biting flies irritate the larger animals, including birds and the wandering herds of caribou or reindeer.

Moss campion

Many Arctic flowers grow in thick, low, rounded clumps called cushions, mixed with other plants such as mosses. This shape helps to protect them from the worst of the cold and the biting winds.

Wet and dry

Boggy tundra supports water-loving plants, while better-drained areas have different, drought-resistant plants. In summer the ground is covered with mosses, lichens, liverworts, grasses, heather, dwarf willows, birch, and other shrubs, and flowers such as dwarf lupins, anemones, buttercups, and gentians.

FRAGILE LAND

Polar soils and the plants which grow on them are very easily damaged. The soil is fragile and the plants grow extremely slowly. A bootprint in an Arctic moss bank, or vehicle tracks across the tundra, may remain clearly visible for dozens of years.

Springtail

As in the Antarctic, the Arctic soil supports tiny insects such as wingless springtails. They feed on all kinds of dead plant matter, helping to return the nutrients to the soil, and so helping with natural recycling. They pass the winter as eggs.

Light Summer, Dark Winter

The North and South Poles are not exactly at the top and bottom of the world. They are slightly to the sides. This is because the Earth is tilted slightly, as it spins around once each day, and goes around the Sun once each year (see page 10). You can use these movements to make a shadow-stick clock that tells both the time of day and the season of the year. You need two pencils, some modeling clay, and a large sheet of card.

1 Stick one pencil in the lump of modeling clay. Stick the lump of clay halfway along one edge of the piece of card, so the pencil is vertical (upright.)

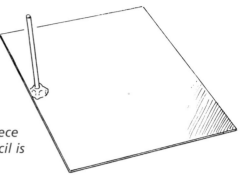

2 Choose a place where you can leave the clock. It should get plenty of sunshine through most of the day, and be safe from the effects of the weather. A large south-facing windowsill (in the Northern Hemisphere) is suitable.

3 On a sunny day, draw the shadows of the pencil as the Sun moves across the sky. (Of course, the Sun is not really moving—it is the Earth that is spinning.) Do this every hour, using a watch or clock to tell the exact time. Mark each shadow drawing with the time and date.

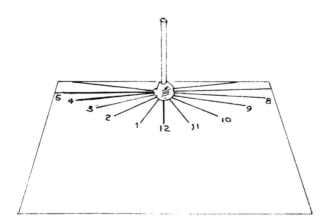

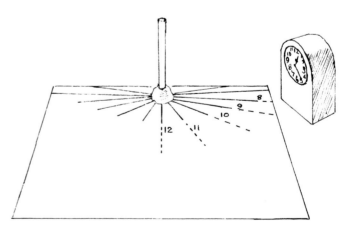

4 Over the next few days, if it is sunny, you can tell the time from the shadow-stick clock. This is how a sundial works.

5 About one month later, on another sunny day, repeat stage 3. Have the lengths of the shadows altered? Do the same after another month. How long are the shadows now? Continue through the year.

When a Compass is Useless

In the area where you live, you can probably find the directions of North and South easily, using a magnetic compass. But the nearer you are to the Poles, the more difficult this becomes. You can see why using a strong bar magnet, a disc of card, Scotch® tape, and a small magnetic compass.

1 The card disc is the world. It should be slightly larger than the bar magnet. Draw the main landmasses onto it, and mark the North and South Poles.

2 Tape the bar magnet onto the middle of the card, pointing North and South. This has an invisible magnetic field around it, like the real Earth.

3 Hold the compass horizontal and the flat Earth just below, upright on its edge. (You need to do this because a compass will not work properly if it is on its side or held at an angle.)

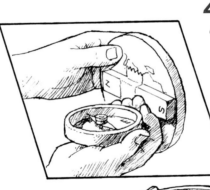

4 Position the flat Earth so the compass is over the Equator. See how the compass works well, lining up with the magnet's field, which is much stronger at this position than the Earth's field. The compass points N–S.

5 Rotate the flat Earth so the compass is over North America or Europe. Does the compass work well now?

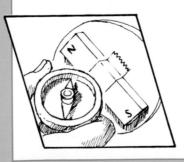

6 Rotate the flat Earth again so the compass is directly over the North Pole. Its needle will probably spin around and settle in a different direction each time. This is because the lines of magnetic force at the Pole are going straight into the Earth. The compass needle cannot align with them (see page 25.)

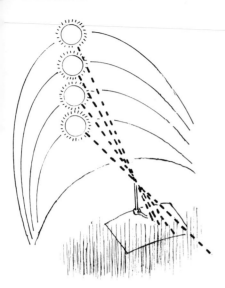

6 The orbit of the Earth around the Sun means that, in many countries, the Sun is lower in the sky during winter. This gives longer shadows. The Sun gradually climbs higher each day towards the summer, producing shorter shadows.

7 This effect becomes more marked as you get nearer the North or South Pole. You can see why, by looking at the diagrams on page 11. What do you think the shadow-stick clock would show through the year, if it was exactly on one of the Poles?

Nesting in the North

In the summer, about 150 species of birds breed in the Arctic. By the winter, more than 140 have gone. They are migrants. To the shores in spring come sea birds like gulls, terns, and divers. However, most of the migrants are freshwater, wetland birds, such as ducks, geese, and swans. They feed and breed on the bogs and pools of the tundra. Most arrive in April, and have usually mated before this. They feed on buds and growing shoots, algae, and a vast range of small animals, on the land and in the freshwater pools and streams.

Most chicks hatch in June and July when food supplies are greatest. As the short Arctic summer draws to a close in August and September, the adult birds and their young must be ready for the long flight south. As the tundra freezes over and winter closes in, only a few birds are left to cope with the darkness and cold.

Arctic (parasitic) skua
A medium-sized skua, this sea bird gets most of its food by pursuing kittiwakes and other gulls, forcing them to drop the items they are bringing back for their own young. They may also take small birds and eggs. They spend winter in the Southern Hemisphere.

Black guillemot
This guillemot breeds on Arctic and sub-Arctic coasts, often nesting in deep crevices in scree (landslide) slopes. It is found in the high Arctic even in winter, when its all-black, summer plumage changes to grey and white. It feeds on fish and seabed-living creatures.

Herring gull
Familiar from Europe and North America, this well-known gull nests hundreds of miles from the sea. It is an all-round scavenger and predator of other sea birds, and their eggs and chicks.

Ptarmigan
In winter, the ptarmigan's plumage is white, to match the snow and ice. This gives camouflage against its predators. In summer, it turns brown to match the rocks, soils, roots, and stems.

Snow goose
The black wingtips of the snow goose identify this otherwise pure-white bird, in flight and on the ground. However, there is also a "blue" variety which has a greyish back and chest.

Whooper swan
The whooper's name comes from its loud, trumpeting call. The female lays 3–5 eggs in a large nest mound of reeds, sedges, and other plant material. The cygnets (young) can fly eight weeks after hatching.

Puffins
The Arctic has three species of puffin. The common puffin is found in the North Atlantic, breeding on Greenland, Iceland, Norway, Bear Island, Novaya Zemlya, and farther south. Horned and tufted puffins live in the Bering Sea area. These birds nest in long burrows dug in the soil.

Wandering the Tundra

Unlike Antarctica, the lands around the Arctic Ocean support some large and powerful herbivores (plant-eaters.) The caribou of North America and the reindeer of Europe and Asia are the same species of animal, although the two groups differ slightly in size and coloring. They spend winter at the forest edges to the south, feeding on shoots, grasses, and lichens. They migrate north in the spring, browsing on the new growth of the tundra plants. Calves are born on this great migration, which may take the herd all the way to the shores of the Arctic Ocean. As the first snows of autumn fall, they move south to their winter feeding grounds.

The smaller herbivores include mice, voles, and lemmings. They can survive and even breed in the icy depths of the Arctic winter—under the snow. The insulating snow blanket protects them from the blizzards and air temperatures above them of −22°F —as cold as a deep freezer. These small bundles of fur make runways under the snow to feeding sites, and "latrines" where they leave their droppings.

Living alone
Adult male caribou often live on their own, except when they join the females at breeding time. The females and young gather together in herds, partly for defense against predators such as wolves.

Mini-herbivores
Tundra plants can be very variable from place to place and season to season. Where plentiful, lemmings, and mice nibble the roots, shoots, and seeds, and breed fast. In some summers, lemming populations "explode" to many times their normal numbers. Their predators, such as owls and foxes, also increase in numbers due to their larger food supply.

54

Musk oxen

The musk ox is the size of a pony. Like the caribou and reindeer, it has only two predators: wolves and humans. Musk ox herds once wandered the tundra all around the Arctic, including northern Asia. Now they are found only in northern Greenland and on the islands of the Canadian archipelago.

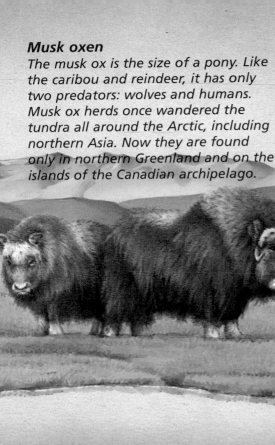

Antlers

Reindeer or caribou are the only type of deer of which the females have antlers, as well as the males. Their wide hooves enable them both to walk on ice without slipping and on soft snow without sinking in. In winter, they shelter and feed in the great conifer forests to the south, scraping away the snow to find plants.

Arctic hare

Like many Arctic creatures, the hare molts its white winter fur and turns brown for the summer. It feeds on juicy summer leaves, shoots, and grasses. During the cold winter, it must survive by digging under the snow for buds, twigs, and shoots.

BLOCKING THE MIGRATIONS?

Caribou and reindeer gather in large herds that need vast grazing areas, because the plants they eat grow so slowly. The building of roads or pipelines across the tundra could block or interrupt their migrations, with disastrous results for herds and tundra.

When the Trans-Alaska Pipeline from the Arctic (north) coast to the Pacific (south) coast was built, there was great concern over its effects on caribou migration. The pipeline was designed to allow the caribou to pass under or over it at certain places. This seems to have worked, and the pipeline has not badly affected the caribou migrations.

Hunters of the Arctic

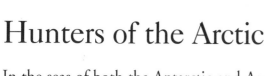

In the seas of both the Antarctic and Arctic, the seal-hunting killer whale is at the top of the food chain. But the Arctic has a seal-hunting land predator, too—the polar bear, king of this icy domain. These great white bears wander over the tundra, swim in the icy seas, and travel to floating icebergs, sea ice, and small islands.

Males usually travel alone, while females are accompanied by their one or two young cubs. The female bear digs a snow den in winter, where the cubs are born in January or February. They emerge from the den with their mother in March or April and stay at her side for two years. Polar bears have been endangered by human hunting, but they are now protected throughout the Arctic.

The other two main land hunters are the wolf and the Arctic fox. Wolves hunt, scavenge, and generally eat what they can. Many track the herds of migrating caribou or reindeer and pick off the old, young, and sick who stray from the main

Wolf
There are many varieties of this species, variously called the grey wolf, timber wolf, and white wolf. They are very adaptable, able to survive in the tundra, forests, grasslands, and mountains. In the Arctic, many wolves are grey or almost white in winter, and brown in summer. They live in large family groups and eat many kinds of food, from caribou to crabs.

Polar bear

The main food of this creamy-white Arctic bear is fish and seals. However, like other bears, it also eats many other things, including roots, shoots, berries, birds, eggs, and small mammals. Polar bears also hang around human settlements and scavenge from refuse dumps, if the opportunity arises. A large male has a head-and-body length of about eight feet, and can easily outrun a caribou over a short distance.

group. The wolf pack hunts together and can run for many hours, tiring any prey.

The Arctic fox feeds mainly on lemmings, which it hunts using an amazing vertical jump to land straight down on top of the victim. Like many Arctic animals, it molts to white in winter, so as to be camouflaged among ice and snow.

Arctic fox

One of the best-adapted mammals to Arctic cold, this fox has small, well-furred ears and furry feet for walking on ice. It preys on small animals, and also scavenges from the leftovers of polar bear kills.

Snowy owl

This is one of the few owls that hunts by day, as well as at dawn, dusk, and in darkness. Its main food is small rodents, such as mice, rats, and lemmings.

Since these prey numbers go up and down wildly, depending on the abundance of plant life, so does the number of owls. In a good year, a pair may raise seven or eight chicks. In a lean year, they may fail to raise one.

Winter Cold: Stay or Go?

There are two main ways of coping with the long darkness and intense cold of Arctic winter. One is to stay and try to survive—sheltering when possible, finding what food is available, and growing even thicker fur, feathers, and a fatty layer under the skin to keep out the cold.

The ptarmigan, in its white, winter plumage, digs in the snow for seeds. The snowy owl constantly searches for rats and lemmings. Musk oxen, insulated against the cold by layers of fat and thick fur, huddle together for protection against winter blizzards, and scratch in the snow to find shoots and lichens. Insects and other small creatures pass the winter as tough-cased eggs that can withstand frost and freezing.

Another option might be to hibernate—but no polar animals truly hibernate, as do the dormice and similar animals of the forests to the south. It is simply too cold in the Arctic, and their bodies would freeze. The second way is to leave and migrate south, like many seals, whales, caribou, and reindeer. Many birds also migrate, flying south to Europe, Asia, and North America.

Birds that go

Arctic terns are amazing travellers. They breed in summer in the Arctic and temperate areas of North America and north-west Europe. Then they fly south for the Antarctic summer, feeding on small fish and krill.

Birds that stay

Among the winter resident birds are the snow bunting (shown here), Lapland bunting, and Arctic and common redpolls. They stay on the tundra, eating seeds which they find on the fringes of the forests.

A whale that goes

Gray whales are found in the Arctic Ocean on either side of the Bering Strait. They are about 42 feet long and feed by stirring the mud on the bottom and then filtering it through their baleen plates. They eat mainly in Arctic waters in summer, then swim south for the winter, along the western coast of North America as far south as California, and down the eastern coast of Asia towards Korea.

Getting about on Snow

Polar animals must be able to move swiftly across soft, deep snow and also hard, slippery ice. Many of the mammals have broad, wide-splayed toes that spread out their body weight, so they do not sink very far into snow, coupled with a furry pad or stiff hairs on the sole, to grip slippery ice. You can test out these designs

SNOWSHOES

1 A snowshoe spreads body weight over a greater area than the sole of an ordinary shoe. This means you should sink less into soft snow, so walking is easier. First, stand in the snow with ordinary shoes. Measure the depth of your print. Is it deeper if you stand on one foot only?

2 Find or make an object that is flat and about the size of a dinner plate to act as a snowshoe. It does not matter if it has small holes. It could be an old tennis racket, a frying pan, or a purpose-made disc of wood. Stand on it in the snow. How deep is the print?

3 Real snowshoes, purpose-made for people, have a pointed design and a mesh or net. This allows the feet to be put down and picked up without too much effort, and it also prevents a build-up of snow on top.

ICE PADS

1 Use the ice in a frozen puddle or water butt. (**Do not walk on the ice of ponds or lakes.**) Put ordinary shoes on your hands and "walk" them across the frozen puddle, feeling how much they can slide.

2 Wrap the shoes in furry or hairy material with fairly stiff bristles, such as a scrap of coarse, long-fiber carpet. Walk them over the ice with your hands. How easily do they slip over the surface?

A polar bear's foot is very broad, to spread its body weight in snow. It has stiff hairs between the pads to grip the ice. It's an excellent two-in-one design!

Surviving in Cold Places

The rocks, ice, and snow of polar lands or mountains look clean, clear, empty and—for some—excitingly inviting. But there are many dangers for the unprepared or the unwary.

The main problem is intense cold, especially when intensified by wind-chill. It can be difficult to find your way in the endless, featureless, white landscape. Snowstorms and white-outs can change the land's features in minutes, so you lose all sense of direction.

Make preparations

If you plan a visit to a cold, snowy, icy place, ensure that you get good advice about the conditions you might encounter. Know the seasonal weather, and check the latest weather forecasts.

Plan and tell others

Do not make your trip too ambitious. Walking through deep snow or across slippery ice can slow your progress to less than one mile per hour. Leave information with the local ranger, or a climbing or countryside center, about where you are going and your time of return.

Never go alone

Always travel in a group, preferably at least four people. One member of the group should know the area and be familiar with polar survival techniques and basic first aid. If you get lost or one person is injured, another can stay while the others get help.

Clothing

Wear approved cold-weather garments such as an anorak, leggings, and ice boots. Have several thinner layers rather than one thick layer. Tight or denim clothing soon chafes and rubs. Up to one-third of body heat is lost from the head, so wear one or two hats that cover all the head except the face. Wear snow goggles to avoid snow glare.

Equipment

Carry extra layers of warm clothing, waterproof and windproof outer garments, first aid kit, survival body-bag (plastic or foil), compass, large-scale maps, whistle, flashlight, and food rations. Use an approved backpack that leaves both arms free.

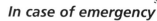

In case of emergency

Discuss and agree a plan of action. The most able and experienced should go for help.

If you are lost, try to find shelter out of the wind. Arrange rocks, colorful items or plant material in a pattern, visible from the air.

The international distress signal is **six whistle blasts or flashlight flashes**, a minute's gap, then six more, and so on.

Frostbite

This usually affects the extremities, mainly fingers, toes, nose, ears, and lips. Thaw the affected part slowly and gently by putting it next to the main body, such as under an armpit, or place it in tepid (**not hot**) water for 15–20 minutes. Always get medical attention as soon as possible.

People at the Poles

The history of humans in the polar regions is very short. There are no people living in the Antarctic, apart from research scientists at the bases. However, the Inuit peoples have lived in the Arctic for thousands of years. Their bodies are better able to tolerate the cold, but whether you are a local person or a visitor to a polar region, extreme care is needed to survive the severe climatic conditions.

An internal body temperature change of no more than 9°F may kill a person. Yet the body can endure variations in air temperature of more than 216°F. Most living quarters in polar regions are purpose-built against the harsh winter conditions.

With stamina, and the right clothing and equipment, plus infinite patience, many activities can be carried out in these high latitudes and sub-zero temperatures. What is more, the scenery, though harsh, can be breathtakingly beautiful.

Skidoo and snowmobile
New methods of transport, and new hunting weapons such as rifles, have changed the way of life for many people in the far north.

Clothing
Normal winter coats are no match for Arctic conditions. Clothes must be specially made and proofed against snow, sleet, rain, and driving winds.

Boats and kayaks
The kayak is traditionally made from seal or caribou skin stretched over a wood or bone frame.

Sled and dog teams
The team of husky dogs can pull a sled for many miles. The very thick fur of these dogs allows them to sleep outside even during bitterly cold nights.

Exploiting Sea and Land

Coal, oil, and natural gas are fossil fuels. Coal is the preserved and fossilized remains of giant ferns and other leafy plants that grew millions of years ago, when the climate was warmer and wetter (see page 20.) Before the continents drifted apart, Antarctica and the land masses around the Arctic had this lush vegetation. So today, some areas have large coal deposits. These are mined for people living farther south. The main coal resources in the Arctic are in Siberia (Vorkuta,) and Svalbard.

Antarctica and South Africa are the only regions in the Southern Hemisphere to have significant quantities of coal. Antarctic coal has never been mined. It may never be in the future, thanks to the protection of the Antarctic Treaty (see page 65.)

Oil and natural gas were also formed by preservation and fossilization over millions of years— mainly from tiny plants, animals and other life forms in the prehistoric oceans. Oil and gas deposits

Mining for minerals
Minerals and metals, in quantities sufficient to be mined, occur throughout the Arctic. They are found in seams and veins in a variety of rock types. They include gold, silver, platinum, uranium, lithium, zirconium, mercury, copper-nickel, cobalt, tungsten, tin, iron, and mica.

Chemical pollution
The killer whale is not currently an endangered species. However, in some areas it is threatened. Chemical pollution may be getting into fish and other animals in the food chains. The pollutants become concentrated as they are eaten by the top predator— the killer whale. The beluga or white whale may be affected in a similar way.

Sealing
In the mid-20th century, sealers killed about 500,000 harp seals each year for their fur coats. Despite all this hunting, the harp seal population remained at about 5 million. The northern fur seal was also widely hunted for its coat. Clubbing harp seals to death was stopped near Canadian shores in 1987 after the European Community banned imports of white harp seal furs. The fall in demand for real fur coats meant that most sealing has now stopped.

Oil disaster

Oil wells have been drilled in the Arctic, and overland pipelines take the crude oil to loading ports, where it is pumped into supertankers.

However, the Exxon Valdez disaster of 1989, when millions of gallons of oil spilled into the seas south of Alaska, showed how dangerous this process can be. Millions of seals, sea birds, and other creatures died.

are widespread throughout the Arctic, mainly along the coasts and shallow seas of northern Canada, Alaska, and Siberia. Millions of tons of oil and gas are obtained by drilling wells, and sent by pipeline and ship to giant refineries. Here they are processed into fuels, lubricants, and hundreds of other products used by the modern world.

Exploitation of all fossil fuels and other minerals is prohibited in Antarctica for 50 years, under the Antarctic Treaty Protocol on Environmental Protection of 1991 (see page 65). But the Arctic region is not so protected. As our world becomes increasingly desperate for fuels and minerals, people move into even colder, more remote regions. They risk disturbing the fragile landscape and wildlife.

Whaling

The introduction of explosive harpoons and fast catching-boats towards the end of the 19th century made big whales a favorite target of the whalers. Nearly 30,000 blue whales were killed in one whaling season in the early 1930s. All mass whaling stopped in 1987. The oceans around Antarctica are now included in the Southern Ocean Sanctuary for whales.

Future Threats

For millions of years, the mixture of gases in the Earth's atmosphere has protected the planet. It has allowed in and kept enough of the Sun's heat to make temperatures fit for life. This is the natural "greenhouse effect." It has also shielded living things from the damaging effects of the Sun's ultraviolet (UV) radiation.

In recent years, scientists have detected changes in the atmosphere. There is a build-up of excess carbon dioxide (CO_2) and other heat-absorbing gases. This may be increasing the natural greenhouse effect and heating the atmosphere, which causes global warming. If this continues, it could change the Earth's surface temperature, with huge consequences. Present estimates predict an average increase of 0.4°F every ten years. This warming would melt some of the polar icecaps and raise sea levels. Many highly populated coastal cities and

Better protection?
In Antarctica, it seems that the world's nations can work together for the good of our nature and wildlife. In 1964, the bringing of foreign plants or animals to Antarctica was banned. Specially protected areas were set up to preserve the range of habitats.

Annual meetings consider scientific advice and decide on catches of fish, squid, and crustaceans in the Southern Ocean. In 1991, all mining was banned in Antarctica for 50 years.

The ozone hole
During the Antarctic winter, strong winds create a cold air column that spirals high into the stratosphere. At temperatures of about −112°F, thin clouds form, upsetting the chemical balance between ozone and the polluting CFC chemicals.

When the Sun returns in spring, a chemical reaction destroys the ozone. In the heat of summer, the air spiral collapses, and more ozone moves in to mend the "hole."

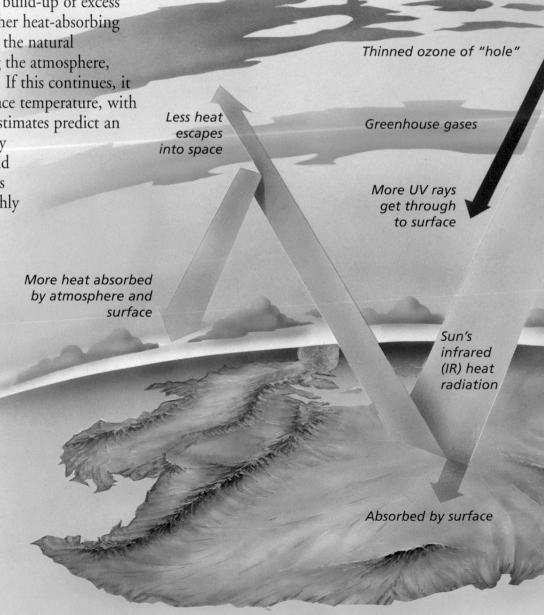

Reflected UV rays

Thinned ozone of "hole"

Greenhouse gases

Less heat escapes into space

More UV rays get through to surface

More heat absorbed by atmosphere and surface

Sun's infrared (IR) heat radiation

Absorbed by surface

The greenhouse effect

Some of the Sun's rays reach the surface and are changed into infrared (IR or heat) radiation. Greenhouse gases like carbon dioxide trap this and prevent it from escaping into space. For millions of years, this natural greenhouse effect has been in balance. But modern activities, such as burning coal and oil in power stations and fuel in vehicles, are producing more carbon dioxide. The greenhouse effect is increasing.

Thinned ozone of "hole"

Ozone layer

Greenhouse gases

regions would be flooded. Whole countries like the Netherlands and Bangladesh may disappear.

Since 1984, scientists have detected a thinning in the natural layer of the gas ozone, especially above Antarctica. Ozone helps to filter out the Sun's harmful UV rays. Too much UV can damage plants, animals, and people, causing conditions such as skin cancer. The ozone is being destroyed by chlorofluorocarbons (CFCs), which are gases from the manufacture of industrial and household items. The world must act to reduce these threats.

THE ANTARCTIC TREATY

In December 1959, twelve nations signed the Antarctic Treaty. They were Argentina, Australia, Belgium, Chile, France, Japan, New Zealand, Norway, South Africa, USA, USSR (now Russia/CIS), and the UK. The Treaty came into force in June 1961. In summary, it says that:

- No military use will be made of Antarctica, although military personnel and equipment may be used for peaceful purposes.

- There will be complete freedom of scientific investigation, and treaty nations will share their plans and scientific results.

- No nation can claim any part of Antarctica as its own.

- Nuclear explosions and nuclear waste disposal are banned from Antarctica.

- All Antarctic stations, and all ships and aircraft supplying Antarctica, shall be open to inspection by observers from any treaty nation.

- Treaty nations will meet at intervals to consider ways of improving the treaty and generally protecting Antarctica.

By 1991, the following additional countries had signed the Treaty: Russia (replacing the USSR), Poland, India, Brazil, Germany, Uruguay, Italy, Peru, Spain, China (People's Republic), Sweden, Finland, North Korea, South Korea, Netherlands, Ecuador, Czech Republic, Denmark, Romania, Bulgaria, Papua New Guinea, Hungary, Cuba, Greece, Austria, Canada, Colombia, Switzerland, and Guatemala.

Measuring the Cold

We usually measure temperatures in units called degrees Fahrenheit (°F). A warm summer's day is about 80°F and a cold winter's day 40°F. Below 32°F, water freezes into ice and we feel bitterly cold. The temperatures in polar regions go far lower than this (see page 11.)

Temperature is measured by a thermometer. Most ordinary thermometers have a silver substance inside them called mercury. This is actually a metal, but it is liquid and flows at normal temperatures. As it becomes warmer, it expands or gets bigger, and pushes further up its narrow tube. (Mercury is very poisonous, so

always handle thermometers with great care.) However, in polar regions, it is sometimes so cold that mercury freezes—it turns into a solid metal. This happens at –38°F, and it could crack the thermometer. So polar thermometers contain another liquid, such as alcohol, which has a much lower freezing point.

You can make your own thermometer to measure the temperature. You need a bottle, a thin and clear tube such as a clear plastic drinking straw, modeling clay, some card, felt pens, Scotch® tape, food coloring, and water.

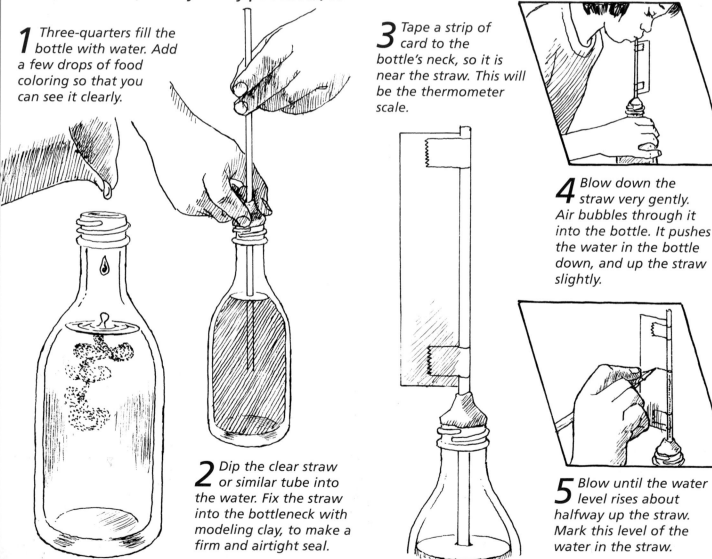

1 Three-quarters fill the bottle with water. Add a few drops of food coloring so that you can see it clearly.

2 Dip the clear straw or similar tube into the water. Fix the straw into the bottleneck with modeling clay, to make a firm and airtight seal.

3 Tape a strip of card to the bottle's neck, so it is near the straw. This will be the thermometer scale.

4 Blow down the straw very gently. Air bubbles through it into the bottle. It pushes the water in the bottle down, and up the straw slightly.

5 Blow until the water level rises about halfway up the straw. Mark this level of the water in the straw.

6 *Put the thermometer in a cold place. The air and water sealed in the bottle become warmer and expand. The water level in the straw rises.*

7 *Put the thermometer in a warm place. The air and water sealed in the bottle become cooler and shrink or contract. The water level in the straw falls.*

8 *You could take the accurate temperature with a real thermometer next to your own one, and mark this on the scale. But you might notice a steady fall in the water level in the straw, over several days. This is due to the water drying out! A real thermometer is sealed at the top, to prevent this happening.*

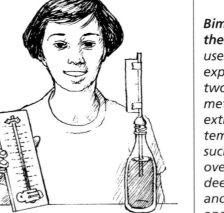

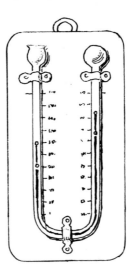

Clinical thermometer for very accurate measurement of body temperature.

Maximum–minimum "greenhouse" thermometer records the highest and lowest temperatures over a time period.

Bimetallic strip thermometer uses different expansions of two different metals—for extreme temperatures such as in ovens, stoves, deep freezers— and the Arctic and Antarctic.

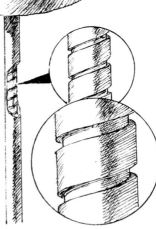

Amazing Facts

- Antarctica is the fifth largest landmass, with an area of 5.5 million square miles—twice the size of Australia. All but 2–3 per cent of it is covered by thick ice throughout the year.

- The ice dome over the Antarctic continent is up to 14,000 feet thick.

- Over one-third of the coastline of Antarctica is covered by 633,200 square miles of floating ice shelves. The Ross Ice shelf alone is about the same size as Texas.

- The Antarctic is also a desert, receiving less than 101 inches of moisture each year. This almost all falls as snow.

The first people to reach the South Pole were from a Norwegian expedition led by Roald Amundsen. They reached the South Pole on December 14, 1911.

British explorer Robert Scott and three others arrived 33 days later, but they all perished on the return journey.

The lowest solid-land point on the Earth's continents is the Bentley Trench under the ice and glaciers of Antarctica. The surface of the bedrock is 8,327 feet below sea level. This compares with the low point of Death Valley, California, at 282 feet below sea level.

The Weddell Sea, off Antarctica, has the clearest sea water in the world. It has been measured as being as clear as purified, distilled water.

The longest glacier in the world is the Lambert Glacier on eastern Antarctica. It is 40 miles wide and 435 miles long. This is almost exactly twice the size of the Grand Canyon in Arizona.

The highest mountain on Antarctica is Vinson Massif, which is 16,066 feet above sea level. However, it appears to be only a few hundred feet high, because of the thickness of the built-up ice around it.

Vostok ice station, near the center of Antarctica, is the coldest place on Earth. Its temperature varies between –128°F in winter and –6°F in summer—still colder than a deep freezer.

The largest iceberg ever came from Antarctica. Its area was 12,000 square miles, being 210 miles long and 60 miles wide. It was tracked in 1956.

If the ice of Antarctica melted, all 27 million billion tons of it, the land of the continent would spring upwards by 1,800 feet, because of the weight removed.

The melted ice of the Antarctic ice cap would raise the sea level worldwide by an estimated 195 feet. This would flood vast low-lying and heavily-peopled lands.

- The Arctic Ocean is the smallest and shallowest of the main oceans. It covers 5.5 million square miles and is an average 4,365 feet deep. Its deepest point is the Nansen Basin, 17,880 feet below sea level.

- In terms of climate, the Arctic is a cold desert. Its average yearly precipitation (rain, snow, and other forms of moisture), apart from a few local exceptions, is less than 10 inches. In northern Greenland, Peary Land is one of the world's driest places, comparable in rainfall to the Sahara.

- 60 per cent of the Arctic is ice-free, and the North American and Eurasian ice-sheets are shrinking.

- Both the Magnetic Poles lie about 800 miles from their geographic counterparts.

- From September to March, the North Pole is in darkness; from March to September, the South Pole is in darkness.

- Permafrost (when the soil is permanently at 32°F or below) freezes the ground to a depth of 1640–2,000 feet. The deepest permafrost known was in Siberia on the upper Viluy River, where it went 4,495 feet deep.

In 1958, the tallest iceberg ever was reported off Greenland. Its highest point was 548 feet above sea level. (The habitable parts of New York's Empire State Building go up to 1,250 feet.)

The most lethal iceberg was the one with which the ocean liner, the Titanic, collided on 14 April 1912. Over 1,100 people died when the ship sank.

The first people to reach the North Pole were supposedly Americans, Robert Peary and Matthew Henson, on April 6, 1909. Some experts say that they could not have done so, since their speed of travel by sled would have been much greater than the speed of other explorers.

The next—or first—people truly to reach the North Pole were Russians. Pavel Geordiyenko and his colleagues got there in April 1948.

In 1946, a floating iceberg or 'island' of ice was seen in the Arctic Ocean. It was not very large, with a surface area of 140 square miles, yet it floated around the ocean for 17 years before melting away.

Find Out More

The best place to begin your search for more information is your school library. Another excellent source of information is your public library. Most newspapers carry regular reports of new advances in science each week. For more information about the plants and animals described in this book, check with your nearest natural history museum or wildlife refuge. They can put you in touch with your local natural history associations as well.

We have listed below a selection of books, organizations, videos, and multimedia programs that will help you learn more about the ARCTIC AND ANTARCTIC.

GENERAL INFORMATION

Alaska Conservation Foundation
    430 W. 7th Avenue
    Suite 215
    Anchorage, AK 99501-3550
American Cetacean Society
    P.O. Box 2639
    San Pedro, CA 90731
    310-548-6279
Center for Environmental Information
    46 Prince Street
    Rochester, NY 14607
    716-271-3550
Center for Marine Conservation

1725 DeSales Street NW
    Suite 500
    Washington, DC 20036
    202-429-5609
Friends of the Sea Otter
    Box 221220
    Carmel, CA 93922
    408-625-3290
Greenpeace
    1436 U Street NW
    Washington, DC 20009
    202-462-1177
National Audubon Society
    950 Third Avenue
    New York, NY 10022
    212-832-3200
National Geographic Society
    17th and M Streets, NW
    Washington, DC 20036
    202-857-7000
National Wildlife Federation
    1400 16th Street NW
    Washington, DC 20036
    202-797-6800
Sierra Club
    100 Bush Street
    San Francisco, CA 94104
    415-291-1600
The Wilderness Society
    1400 Eye Street NW
    Washington, DC 20005
    202-842-3400
World Wildlife Fund
    1250 24th Street NW
    Washington, DC 20037
    202-293-4800

BOOKS

Arctic & Antarctic Barbara Taylor
    Knopf/Random House
    ISBN 0-679-87257-4
The Amateur Naturalist Charles C. Roth
    Franklin Watts ISBN 0-531-11002-8

Ecology Projects for Young Scientists
    Martin J. Gutnik
    Franklin Watts ISBN 0-531-04765-2
Glaciers and Ice Caps Martyn Bramwell
    Franklin Watts ISBN 0-531-10178-9
The Living Planet: A Portrait of the Earth
    David Attenborough
    Little Brown ISBN 0-316-05748-7
The Power of Ice Ruth Radlauer and
    Lisa S. Gitkin
    Childrens ISBN 0-516-07839-9
Science Nature Guides: Fossils
    Thunder Bay Press
    ISBN 1-85028-262-5
Science Nature Guides: Mammals
    Thunder Bay Press
    ISBN 1-57145-016-5
Water for the World Franklyn M. Branley
    Crowell ISBN 0-690-04172-1

VIDEOS

National Geographic Society
    produces a wide range of wildlife and
    geographical videos
Time-Life Video
    produces a wide range of wildlife and
    geographical videos

MULTIMEDIA

3D Atlas Electronic Arts
The Big Green Disc Gale Research
Eyewitness Encyclopedia of Nature
    Dorling Kindersley
Fourth & Fifth Grade Science
    Sierra Education
Global Learning Mindscape
Multimedia Animals Encyclopedia
    Applied Optical Media
Picture Atlas of the World
    National Geographic Society
Survey of the Animal Kingdom
    Zane Publishing
A World Alive Softline

Glossary

atmosphere The layer of air around the Earth, which becomes thinner with increasing height, until it fades to nothing in outer space.

aurora borealis or australis Glowing curtains and shimmering shapes of lights high in the atmosphere, caused by energy and particles coming from the Sun.

blubber A thick layer of fat just under the skin of an animal, to keep in body warmth and insulate against cold surroundings.

carnivore An animal that eats other animals, usually a hunter that feeds on meat or flesh.

continental drift The movement of the main continents or landmasses around the surface of the Earth, carried on TECTONIC PLATES.

crevasse A crack or gap in a body of ice such as a GLACIER or ICE BERG.

current A body or volume of water that moves in relation to the water around it.

dormancy When a living thing remains still and inactive, as though asleep, to save energy and survive bad conditions. Aestivation and hibernation are types of dormancy.

evaporation When a liquid turns into a vapor or gas. Liquid water evaporates or "dries" into invisible water vapor.

food chain A list or sequence of who eats what, beginning with plants and ending with the top carnivore. In nature, many food chains usually link to form food webs.

glacier A mass of ice, formed from snow, which moves very slowly down a mountain.

habitat A type of place or surroundings in the natural world, often named after the main plants that grow there. Examples are a conifer forest, a grassland such as a meadow, a desert, a pond, or a sandy seashore. Some animals are adapted to only one habitat, like limpets on rocky seashores. Other animals, like foxes, can survive in many habitats.

herbivore An animal that eats plant food, such as shoots, stems, leaves, buds, flowers, and fruits.

ice berg A mountain of ice that has broken off from a GLACIER and is floating in the sea.

ice shelf A layer of ice extending from the shore of a land mass and floating on the surrounding sea.

meltwater the freshwater which comes from melting ice and snow and mingles with the seawater.

migration In nature, a journey which is usually long-distance and carried out regularly by certain animals, to find better conditions for feeding or breeding.

permafrost Land where the ground is always frozen at a temperature of 32°F or lower.

plankton Mass of small plants (phytoplankton) and animals (zooplankton) drifting near the surface of seas or lakes.

precipitation The overall name for water reaching the surface of the Earth, including rain, sleet, snow, frost, and dew.

tectonic plate One of the giant curved plates that makes up the outer surface of the Earth, and which moves or drifts in relation to the other plates.

tree line The edge of the woods and forests, which marks the place where the climate becomes too cold and/or dry for trees to grow.

tundra Treeless land, mostly in the Northern Hemisphere, covered by small, low plants, where the climate is too cold for trees to grow.

zooplankton see PLANKTON.

Index

Adélie penguin, 41
Age of Dinosaurs, 21, 22–23
Albedo, 10
Amundsen–Scott Station, 9
Animal life: Antarctic, 22–23, 31
    basic food, 32
Animal life: Arctic, 45, 48–49
    coping with winter, 58
    extent of, 6
    food source, 45
    hunters, 56–57
    moving on ice/snow, 59
    reading tracks, 44
    Southern Ocean, 8, 33
    food source, 33
    tundra, 49, 54–55
    see also Dinosaurs;
      Insulation, and
      specific animals
Antarctic Bottom Layer, 14, 15
Antarctic Convergence, 8, 14
Antarctic Divergence, 15
Antarctic Peninsula, 9, 13
    bird colonies, 42–43
Antarctic Treaty, 63, 65
Antarctica, 8–9
    age of, 21, 22
    ban on exploitation, 62–64
    highest mountain, 21
    humans in, 61
    ice-free area, 30
    islands near, 9
    link with South America, 21
    movements of, 20–21
    ozone hole, 64–65
    scientific bases, 9
    seal species, 38–39
    study of ice from, 27
    surface area, 8, 21
    see also Southern Ocean
"Antifreeze," animal, 32
Arctic: coping with winter in, 58
    exploitation of resources
      62–63
    humans in, 61
    ice-free land, 48

link with Atlantic Ocean, 21
surface area, 21
what it is, 6, 7
Arctic ducks, 7
Arctic fox, 56, 57
Arctic hare, 55
Arctic Ocean, 7
    deepest point, 21
Atmosphere: effect on solar
    wind, 16, 17
    movement in, 12
    see also Winds
    studying history of, 27
Auroras, 16, 17

Baleen whales, 36, 37, 46, 47
Beluga, 46
    threat to, 62
Birds: Arctic:
    breeding in, 52–53
    coping with winter, 58
    food source, 49
    types of, 52
    insulation, 35
    Southern Ocean, 8, 42–43
    "tube-nose" group, 42
    see also Penguins
Blizzards, 28
Blubber, 35
Blue-eyed shag, 42
Bottlenose whale, northern, 46
Bowhead whale, 46, 47
Brown skua, 43

Camouflage, winter, 52
Caribou, 54
    antlers, 55
    migration, 55
    predators, 56–57
Carnivores, Antarctica, 31
Chinstrap penguin, 40, 41
Climate, 10–11, 12–13
    Age of Dinosaurs, 22–23
    historical changes in, 6
Clothing for cold weather, 60
Cod, Antarctic, 33
Cold, measuring, 19
Compass, useless, 51
Coriolis effect, 12, 13
Crabeater seal, 38

Crevasses, 26
    ice formation in, 28
Currents: Arctic Ocean, 7
    circulation of nutrients, 45
    Southern Ocean, 14–15
    circulation of nutrients, 32

Desert, polar region, 12–13, 30,
    48–49
Diatoms, 32, 33
Dinosaurs, fossil evidence, 21,
    22–23
Diving ability: seals, 39
    whales, 37
Dove prion, 42
Down-welling, 14

Echolocation, seals, 39
Elephant seal, southern , 38
Emperor penguin, 40, 41

Fin whale, 37
"Flying," underwater, 40
Food chain, Southern Ocean,
    32, 33
Fritillary, Arctic, 48
Frostbite, 60
Fulmar, Antarctic, 43
Fur seals:
    northern, 47
    southern, 38, 39
Fur trade, 62

Gas extraction, 62–63
Gentoo penguin, 41
Geographic poles, 24
Giant petrel, southern, 42
Glaciers, 27
Gnats, Arctic, 49
Gray whales, 58
"Greenhouse effect," 64–65
Greenland:
    ice cover, 26–27
    study of ice from, 27
Greenland–Norwegian Gap, 7
Guillemot, Black, 52

Harp seals, 47
    threat to, 62
Herbivores: Antarctic, 31

Arctic, 54
Herring gull, 52
Humpback whale, 37, 46

Ice: amount of fresh water in, 13
    breaking through Arctic, 6
    effect of light reflection, 18
    effect on temperatures, 10
    studying, 27
    types of, 26
Ice, measuring power of, 29
Ice Ages, 22
Ice caps:
    "greenhouse effect" and, 64
    thickness/weight of, 26–27
"Ice cores," 27
Ice fish, 32
Ice flower, 28
Ice garden, 28
Ice pads, 59
Ice sheet, Antarctica, 8
    formation of, 26
Ice sheet, Arctic:
    formation of, 26–27
    water under, 6
    extent during Ice Ages, 20
Ice shelves, 9, 26
Icebergs: what they are, 27
Icicles, 28
Insects, Arctic, 49
    coping with winter, 58
Insulating layers, 35
Insulation: Arctic winter, 58
    whales and seals, 35, 46
Inuit peoples, 61

Kayaks, 61
Killer whales, 36, 56
    threat to, 62
King penguin, 40

Leads, 26
Lemmings, 54
    predators, 57
Leopard seal, 38, 39
Lichens: Antarctic, 30
    Arctic, 49
Light: curtains of, 16, 17
    effect of ice crystals, 18
    water plants and, 32

Magnetic poles, 24–25
  reversal of, 24–25
Mawson Base, Antarctica, 11
McCormick's skua, 43
McMurdo Base, Ross Island, 9
Meltwater: currents and, 14–15
  tundra pools, 48
Midges, Arctic, 49
Migration: effect of roads and
  pipelines on, 55
  from Arctic winter, 58
  whales, 36–37, 46
Mining, 62
Minke whale, 37
Mirages, polar, 18
Moon halo, 18
Mosquitoes, Arctic, 49
Moss campion, 49
Mosses, 30
Mountains: Antarctica, 8, 9
  Arctic, 6
Musk oxen, 55
  and Arctic winter, 58

Narwhal, 46
North Pole:
  magnetic pole and, 24–25
  temperature at, 11
Northern Lights, 16, 17
Norwegian basin, 21

Oil extraction, 62–63
  disasters, 63

Pangaea (supercontinent), 21
"Pancake" ice, 27
Penguins, 40–41
  sub-Antarctic, 40, 41
Permafrost, 7
Petrels, 42
  defence, 42
Phytoplankton, 33
  in Southern Ocean, 33
Plankton:
  whale eating method, 36
  in Arctic Ocean, 45
  yearly cycle, 34
  see also Phytoplankton;
  Zooplankton
Plant life: Antarctica, 30–31

flowers, 31
  fossil remains, 22, 23
  Arctic, 48–49
    polar desert, 49
    tundra, 48–49
  Southern Ocean, 32, 33
Polar bears, 56, 57
  walking on ice, 59
Polar regions:
  comparisons between, 21
  extent of, 6
  history, 20–21
  why they are cold, 10–11
Poles: number of, 24
  see also Geographic poles;
  Magnetic poles
Pollutants/pollution: effect of
  water movement on, 15
  method of studying, 27
  oil spills/slicks, 63
  threat from chemicals, 62
  see also "Greenhouse effect"
Polynyas, 26
Poppy, Arctic, 48
Precipitation, annual total,
  12–13
Ptarmigan, 52
  and Arctic winter, 58
Puffins, 53

Reindeer: antlers, 55
  migration, 55
  predators, 56–57
Reindeer moss, 48
Ringed seal, 46
Rocks: magnetic record, 24–25
  types in Antarctica, 22
Rodinia (supercontinent), 20
Ross seal, 38, 38

Sea bed, Arctic, 6
Sea ice: flows and ridges, 26
  formation of, 27
  seasonal melting, 11
Sea smoke, 13
Sealing, 62
Seals: Antarctic, 38–39
  Arctic, 46–47
    coping with winter, 58
Seasons: causes of, 10, 12

winter, 11
Shadow-stick clock, 50–51
Shorelines:
  history/characteristics, 20, 21
Skidoo, 61
Skuas, 43
  Arctic, 52
Sled/dog teams, 61
Snow:
  protection for herbivores, 54
  tracks in, 44
  what it is, 28
"snow blindness," 28
Snow bunting, 58
Snow den, 56
Snow goose, 53
Snow petrel, 42
Snowflakes, 28
Snowmobile, 61
Snowshoes, 59
Snowy owl, 57
  and Arctic winter, 58
Soil: Arctic, 48
  fragility of, 49
  Antarctic, 30–31
Solar wind, glow of, 16, 17
South Georgia (Island), 9
  penguin colonies, 41
South Georgia Ridge, 21
South Orkney Islands, 9
South Sandwich Island, 9
South Shetland Islands, 9
Southern Lights, 16, 17
Southern Ocean, 8
  effect of prevailing winds
  14–15
  nutrients/fertility, 32, 33
Sperm whales, 37, 46
Springtail, 49
Squid, 34
"sundogs," 18
Sunrise, sunless, 18
Survival:
  clothes and equipment, 60
  guidelines, 60

Temperatures: and windchill, 13
  Antarctica, 11
  at Antarctic
  Convergence/Divergence, 15

effect on plant life, 49
  how cold is cold, 11
  humans and, 61
  lowest/highest recorded, 11
  ocean layers, 15
Terns, Antarctic, 43
Thermometer, making, 66–67
Toothed whales:
  Antarctic, 36
  Arctic, 46
  largest, 37
Tracks, reading, 44
"Tree line," 6
Tundra, 48–49
  animal species, 54–55

Vinson Massif, 9
Vostock station, Antarctica, 11

Walrus, 45
Water beetle, 48
Water:
  movement in oceans, 14–15
  nutrients/carbon dioxide in,
  32
  see also Ice
Weather:
  circulation of systems, 12–13
  extent of Arctic, 6
  see also Climate; Windchill
Weddell seal, 38–39
Whales:
  Antarctic, 36–37
  Arctic, 46, 47
    coping with winter, 58
  deepest diver, 37
  insulation, 35
  threat from pollution, 62
Whaling, 63
"Whiteout," 28
Whooper swan, 53
Wilson's storm petrel, 42–43
Windchill, 13
Winds:
  northern patterns, 13
  southern patterns, 12
  see also Coriolis effect
Wolf, 56–57

Zooplankton, 33